TEENAGE BELIEFS

'We are here to live our lives for God... by the pattern Jesus showed us.'

Educationalists David Day and Philip May felt that the negative stereotype of the rebellious teenager was inaccurate. Their in-depth survey of teenage Christians is both enlightening and refreshing.

DAVID DAY is Senior Lecturer in Education at the University of Durham, where he specializes in the teaching of Religious Education. Before taking up his present post he taught for fifteen years in schools in London and Nottingham.

PHILIP MAY is Reader in Education at the University of Durham, where he has taught for the last thirty years. He is the author of several other books, dealing mainly with the topic of Christian education.

Acknowledgments

We should like to thank all the sixty-seven young people who so willingly gave up their time to talk with us, and answered our questions so openly. Every one of them is quoted somewhere in the book and we are most grateful for their co-operation.

We should also like to thank the British and Foreign Schools Society, who kindly gave a grant to help towards the cost of the research on which this book is based.

Teenage Beliefs

David Day
Philip May

A LION PAPERBACK
Oxford · Batavia · Sydney

Text copyright © 1991 David Day and Philip May
This edition copyright © 1991 Lion Publishing

Published by
Lion Publishing plc
Sandy Lane West, Oxford, England
ISBN 0 7459 1963 4
Albatross Books Pty Ltd
PO Box 320, Sutherland, NSW 2232, Australia
ISBN 0 7324 0280 8

First edition 1991

British Library Cataloguing in Publication Data
Day, David
   Teenage beliefs.
   1. Great Britain. Christian adolescents.
   I. Title   II. May, Philip
   208.350941
   ISBN 0 7459 1963 4

Printed in Great Britain
by Cox and Wyman

Contents

1
Familiar Strangers

God, that's all I've got to keep my mind on.

There is no shortage of negative stereotypes about adolescents. In fact the media seem to have a vested interest in emphasizing the shocking, the bizarre and the violent. The headlines reflect this: 'New gambling craze shocks parents'; 'Teenage gang attacks lone PC'; 'Girl, 10, led teenage terror'; 'Rat pack hooligans'; 'Yobbery with violence—a study of Chelsea supporters'. No wonder a Bradford University survey concluded, 'According to our daily press a typical adolescent is a sporting youngster, criminally inclined, likely to be murdered or injured in an accident.'

Unfortunately some of the mud sticks, with the result that 'everyone knows what teenagers are like'. We see them 'hanging round leisure centres annoying the attendant', or 'fighting at bus stops on their way to school'. They are 'always rioting at football matches', 'up to no good in the woods' or 'vandalizing phone booths'. Some unfortunate people actually have one or two in the house, where they pillage the fridge, demand money with menaces, turn bedrooms into rubbish tips and treat the place like a hotel.

We also know, of course, that reality does not always match the stereotype. We meet enough teenagers who are idealistic, romantic, eager to change the world, caring, vulnerable, involved in good causes, refreshingly honest, open, good humoured and enthusiastic to make us adjust our prejudices. So why do the prejudices persist?

One intriguing answer has been put forward by John Mitchell, an American psychologist. He has suggested that adult society is drawn to the negative image of the adolescent because basically 'we don't like them'.[1] Bad news about teenagers is something most adults deep down want to hear.

It is not difficult to see the sense in this theory. In the first instance, some adolescents can seem hostile and threatening. Many adults have had close encounters of a terrifying kind—at a football match, in a shopping arcade, at a bus stop. The stories of classroom violence seem all too possible when one is faced with the provocative behaviour, threatening language and aggressive dressing of some young people. A motorist fumes as a youth saunters across the road in front of his car, two fingers up, at a pace calculated to annoy. The declaration of hostility is apparent.

Second, adolescents bewilder and mystify us. Their language, clothes, interests, pursuits, attitudes, tastes, magazines and TV programmes are part of a world to which adults have little access. An attractive seventeen-year-old dresses down in clothes she bought for ten pence from the Oxfam shop—to the despair and bewilderment of her parents. Teenagers seem like creatures from another planet. A reporter on the *Sunday Times* did a study of young people for the colour supplement. She was surprised to find her friends expressing alarm and sympathy and asking, 'What are they like?'—'as though one had returned from a long stay with the Marsh Arabs'.

Third, it is possible that some dislike of adolescents is born of envy. They have freedom and choice with little responsibility—or so it seems. They have more money than they know what to do with and do not have to worry about mortgages or gas bills. They can lie in bed till noon without having to get to work by 8.30. One girl spoke to us soon after a blazing row with her mother, ostensibly about what clothes were suitable for a disco. 'Why do you think your mother reacted so strongly?' we asked. With a rare insight she answered, 'I think she was remembering a time when she had the pick of the boys. And now she's stuck with my dad.'

8

Fear, bewilderment and envy are powerful emotions. It is easy to see how they can fuel prejudice. Yet there is a substantial body of opinion which believes that the stereotypical view of adolescents is an amalgam of myths, and that such negative assessments are unfair to the vast body of young people. If adolescents could speak for themselves, the argument runs, then adults would begin to get a far different picture.

This book is a very small contribution to the business of letting adolescents speak for themselves. It is about teenagers who get religion—specifically the Christian religion. One of its basic presuppositions is that adolescents are normal human beings. They pursue answers to the same questions as the rest of humanity: 'Do I like myself?' 'Can I manage?' 'Am I competent?' 'Am I an individual?' Their agendas are human agendas. Our concern is that we should be able to hear them and that we should allow them to speak freely and at length.

For example, here is part of Gary's attempt to find his own faith position and break away from the tightly knit community to which his parents belong:

'About three weeks after that I left the community. I don't regret the decision I made. What I've done is wrong but basically I've been doing what I wanted to do, and also, there's a large part of "I've done it and nobody else wants me to do it." In fact everyone says, "Don't do it." So I say, "Blow, I'm going to do it." There's a certain satisfaction in doing what you know you shouldn't. Christianity's sort of to me...well, I'm wearing a coat but there's lots of blotches on the coat, do you see what I mean? It's sort of stubbornly sitting there. It's left its mark.'

Christine decided for herself that she would not mix with an older woman who dabbled in the occult. She then had to learn to handle the effects of that decision:

'So she never got into contact with us for ages, really not until about a month ago. And then she phoned up and she was really going mad with us. She said I needed my head examining and I should be put in a mental home and she was going to come up and

9

see my mam and dad about religion and everything...really trying to get at us.'

Emma was working through a problem common to many adolescents, that of a negative self-image. It was her belief that her new-found faith had solved everything in a moment. However, as we listen to her we may hear the uncertainty beneath the ringing conviction:

'I used to be really down on myself—even used to get into trouble for it. That was because I was overweight and had no nice clothes—all that sort of thing. Now I feel that doesn't matter any more. I'm sorry... God, that's all I've got to keep my mind on. I used to long for new clothes... I'm not saying I don't now...but the things I used to worry about, I don't worry about now. Well, I do now and then but I just give it over to God and it subsides. And then it comes back and I say, "Oh, I don't want to know."'

A young Roman Catholic found himself caught between faith and friendship. He sensed that he was heading for disaster but at that point the old formulae were inadequate to meet his personal need for love and acceptance:

'I felt I was having a nervous breakdown but didn't. I drank such a lot, which was totally against my Christian beliefs. I spent, for two weeks, most of my time drunk. And the circle of friends that I met, half of them were gay and the other half were sleeping around...but it didn't matter. None of them had any Christian morals. They were using one another. The theatre world is horrible. They use one another. And I felt lost. I thought, "If this is where I am, I'm not going to survive. My faith is not going to survive here and I ought to move out of it. How can I carry on here?" But my need for people was greater. I couldn't survive in just the knowledge that God, Jesus, had been here. That wasn't good enough.'

Here are real people trying to make sense of the spiritual dimension to their lives and to integrate it with everything else that is happening to them. Many of the accounts we heard were equally powerful and moving, sometimes confident and joyful, sometimes hesitant and uncertain. They shed a vivid light on the tasks, pressures, challenges and possibilities of growing up and for this reason we think that they are of interest to all kinds of people, whether teenage or adult, religious or otherwise. However, we believe that there are three particular groups of people for whom the book is especially relevant.

First, there are parents who are themselves not religious. A teenage conversion in the family may set up all kinds of anxieties. Has our son or daughter joined the Moonies? Will she start seeing visions in the style of Bernadette? Or give up doing his school examinations in order to become a monk? The mother who said to her son when she was told of his conversion, 'That's nice, dear, but don't let it get too serious,' was expressing the fear that a religious faith might entail the loss of everything the family thought important. Such parents naturally want to know what has happened to their child. They fear that religious faith is neurotic; they have heard of wild goings on—exorcisms, speaking in tongues and the like. They worry that normal teenage development will somehow be perverted into something altogether too intense and unhealthy. What goes on at prayer meetings? Why should a normal teenager want to spend New Year's Eve at a communion service? or go on a youth pilgrimage? or get up early in the morning to pray?

The second group we have in mind are parents who are Christian and know the world of the church. Even here there may be anxiety and bewilderment since it is not unknown for the adolescent to choose (deliberately? perversely?) a denomination other than the parental one. But given the more usual situation, that of parent and child in the same church, we believe that our accounts may help in a different way. One parent who listened to a report we gave on the interviews remarked, 'I'm sure my son wouldn't speak like that.' Now it is possible that she was right. But an alternative explanation is that her son does not speak freely and openly about his view of the Christian faith in front of her. After all, it is fairly common for teenagers to become uncommunicative with their parents about many important matters. It is our hope that the in-depth and honest responses of a number of teenage Christians may give Christian parents an insight into the unvoiced values and attitudes of their own children.

Our third group comprises those involved with youth in the church, both leaders and ordinary members. It used to be said that children and young people were the church of tomorrow. Recent thinking has been concerned to assert that they are very much a part of the church of today. But the move to give young people their proper place in the church is accompanied by a growing fear that large numbers of them will not be there tomorrow anyway. This kind of anxiety led to the research project sponsored by the Church of England Board of Education which was eventually published as *Young People's Beliefs*.[2] The preface to that report notes that 'young people are wide open to belief but not in a way which the church has traditionally recognised' and that 'analysis of a situation must necessarily be the basis of any serious attempt at mission'. Ministers, youth leaders and other church members may find as a result of reading these accounts that they have more in common with the young people in their church than they at first suspected.

The chief reason for listening to these accounts is to understand young Christians and young people better. For adults they may have quite another effect, however. As we read their stories we begin to recognize something of ourselves in them. The recognition sometimes causes amusement, sometimes impatience and sometimes pain. We are anxious on their behalf because we see them making the same sort of critical decisions we had to make. We occasionally experience a kind of wistful longing, a hope that they will get it right where we got it wrong. This may also explain moments of disapproval as the adult wants to mould the adolescent in his or her own image and finds the disparity in behaviour or outlook vaguely threatening. We have found that these interviews frequently provoke a dialogue in us. The dialogue is often illuminating and occasionally disturbing. It represents unfinished business as the adult and the half-forgotten adolescent within ourselves begin to talk to one another again.

References

[1]John J. Mitchell, *Adolescent Psychology*, Holt, Rinehart and Winston, 1979, p.192.

[2]Bernice Martin and Ronald Pluck, *Young People's Beliefs*, General Synod Board of Education, 1976.

2
Changed Lives

Why can't I be mad and wild and free?

Before I was a Christian I didn't really think there was any purpose in life. I thought life just went on.

We should like to introduce the young people we interviewed at a point where we think most of them might say people should begin to get to know and understand them. This is the point where they differed from so many of their contemporaries, the area of faith. We chose to talk to them because they said they were Christians, and if they really were different, or were changing, then their beliefs should be the main cause.

It is a common experience to hear people say that we live in an age of change. Teenagers certainly seem to welcome variety and like doing things that are different from the usual daily run. Some changes have more lasting effects than others. The New Testament suggests that becoming a Christian is the most radical experience anyone can have. It uses pretty startling descriptions such as 'being born again', and 'passing from death to life'.

So how did the sixty-seven young people we interviewed see the difference in themselves that admitting to be Christians in their own right had caused? Did they see any difference at all? Had they changed in the way they thought, felt and acted? Were such changes mere passing fancies or something ongoing and more permanent? We asked them to tell us about seven distinct areas of their lives, and to say whether being a Christian made a difference there for them.

14

They all claimed that they did detect differences in themselves. This was the case whether becoming a Christian had been for them a gradual growing experience or an event which took place at a specific time in their lives. Sometimes in some areas they saw no change. But where they thought they did see differences, they gave us plenty of illustrations.

Behaviour

The first question was, 'Does being a Christian make a difference to the way you behave?'

We were given 108 examples of differences, some of the young people telling us of several instances, and many speaking of the same kind of thing. In the course of the lengthy interviews we conducted, further relevant illustrations were given as part of answers to other questions. Apart from one girl and one boy who answered, 'Not much,' and did not elaborate further, the interviews provided a total of twenty-four different points. Sometimes a point was made by only one person. These unique answers included the comments 'I'm quieter', 'I'm less lazy', 'I avoid telling lies', 'I'll only now go out with a Christian girl', 'I refuse to sleep with boys', 'I listen more', 'I'm less selfish', and 'Now I honour my parents'. In contrast, twenty young people said they now were much more self-controlled, and a similar number felt they were more considerate and tolerant. Sixteen stated that they now always tried to test their actions against their Christian beliefs and teaching. Such, at least, were their current perceptions of themselves.

In the course of the interviews, many acknowledged that being a Christian had given them different standards for behaviour. They all tried to 'obey the commandments' and follow the teaching of their church. Derek told us, 'I'm more conscious of what's right and wrong when tempted—what I should and what I shouldn't do.' Similarly, Hilary emphasized that 'it makes you think much more about what you are doing'.

Mary explained:

'*Sometimes there's ways you want to behave and you realize there's ways that Jesus would prefer you to behave. I find when I give the loving answer, rather than the selfish or nasty answer, it's so much more peaceful and fulfilling, especially in our home.*'

Fifteen-year-old Laura was both brief and frank:

'*You think about the sort of person you should be. Often I'm not, but I try to be.*'

A number of those questioned admitted that living up to Christian standards of behaviour was a struggle. Let Sally speak for all of them:

'*It's funny. Sometimes I sit there and think, "Oh, why can't I just go out and go mad and just do what everyone else is doing?" I say it, and I think it, but in my heart—do you know what I mean?—I think, "Why do I think like this? Why have I got these morals? Why have I got this set of rules to live with? Why can't I be mad and wild and free?" In a worldly sense, I suppose. Then I'm saying it and thinking it, but I don't really want to. In my heart I know I want to be a Christian and I've got to live by these rules. I know "got to" sounds bad. I mean, I want to. I do want to, even though there are moments. It's never for long. It's just a few minutes when you're low, when things are happening, and you think, "Oh dear, why not?" But it never lasts for long. And then you suddenly think, "Why was I thinking like that?"*'

When it came to living out their Christian lives, many said that they did now think before acting. Alan's remark is fairly typical. He said, 'I've got to see if a situation is one I can go into as a Christian.' Two other boys commented that they were now 'able to walk away from aggro and ignore it', and many of both sexes said it had stopped them swearing and gossiping as well as changing where they went. Mandy stressed the difference it made to her in what she called the little things:

'*There's lots of little things. They don't really matter, but they do. Such as when you're saying horrible things about your* brother and then you realize that's stupid and you shouldn't really think things like that. Or I don't want to do something but I know I should, so I do. I don't know what I'd be like if I didn't have this consciousness behind me that God doesn't want me to do that, or God will be thinking, "That's not very nice." Not all the time. Temptation keeps coming in. But it's just those little things that seem to matter.'

Melanie's behaviour and attitude had changed considerably:

'Before I became a Christian I was a recluse more or less, during the daytime especially. I just wanted to be on my own. I used never to look people in the face. Now I'm willing to go and help people decorate or look after the kids. At the moment, I'm still scared of getting a job. I prefer to help people.'

Barry's radical change included his appearance:

'When I become a Christian and I had all my hair dyed green and orange and that, I says to myself, It's not going to be very nice if people say to me, "Are you a Christian?" and I'm standing there with rips in my clothes, safety pins all over, and my hair dyed, 'cos they'll say, "If that's a Christian, I don't want anything to do with that." So I changed.'

In addition, he 'got a different set of mates', and stopped glue-sniffing.

We also think it worth quoting Graham's answer. He assured us he'd changed 'loads':

'I mean, if I saw an old woman walking down the street, or a cripple, then I'd have sneered at them. Which is sick, when you think back. But I wouldn't dream about doing it now. I used to pull the legs off spiders and things. Very stupid thing. But now you think that's something that's living, a part of God's creation. You think how beautiful it is. And you'll be walking along in the countryside and you think this is what it must have been like in the beginning. Much closer it brings you to God.'

The people interviewed also said their feelings about their behaviour had changed or were changing. As well as exercising more self-control and becoming more patient, many acknowledged that they now reacted differently in

17

various situations, and were much more aware of the effect on others of what they did. Barbara's comments are typical:

'*I've become more patient. I've got more self-control. I'm more prepared to accept people for who they are and not what they look like, and things like that. With my parents not being Christians, that's really difficult at times, and a difficult place to be. I often feel provoked a lot of the time. I think I represent a challenge to them, and I think they want to see me get angry, because they sort of feel they have achieved something. So I find it...my sister particularly provokes me and it's very hard to be patient. I mean you last so long and then you eventually burst. But I must admit it's taking longer. They need to do it more now, to get me to go, to get me angry. But sometimes I give in. Now if you get into an argument and it's just a senseless argument, I just say I'm not prepared to argue about it, as it's no good. Whereas before I'd have taken up the challenge, now I'm not prepared to argue, 'cos it's not achieving anything.*'

Paula also told us that she found trying to be a Christian at home was hard:

'*At home, at home, it is difficult. Being a Christian home you are expected to be good, and being a Christian once you are converted does not always make a difference, because you have been brought up like that. I would say it was difficult at home to show Christian attitudes because they say, Oh look, they've suddenly gone really really religious, not just religious. Really really. That I find difficult sometimes.*'

But Paul, in general, felt able to be more positive:

'*Well, as far as the way I behave, I feel more confident, definitely. I can now go into something without worrying, because I'm safe with my faith.*'

Sixteen-year-old Caroline's answer aptly rounds off this section, not least because so many of those we questioned would echo what she said:

'*I wouldn't say that since I became a Christian I'd become so angelic. I still experience what other people experience, but with the Lord being there, I can ask him to help me, and he does, so it goes no further than that.*'

Work

Our question about whether being a Christian made any difference to their attitude to their work, and to the way they did their work, was broad in scope. The question applied to their studies, their participation in domestic chores and to their part-time and full-time employment, where relevant. Many said they now worried much less about their studies, examinations and jobs. The anxiety was reduced, or had disappeared, because they felt they were no longer bearing all the burdens themselves. And we were repeatedly told that now they wanted what they did to be used for the glory of God and to honour him.

One eighteen-year-old enjoying his first full-time work replied, 'Yes, I feel I've got to give my best to God, so you can't really cut corners. I have more commitment now to what I do.' Steve, also eighteen but unemployed, having been made redundant a year before, asserted, 'I'd not take a job unless the Lord said, "Take it." And I'd know, if I had peace about the job, in my heart and mind.' Nick, sixteen, told us he grumbled much less about his school studies. 'I think there should be less complaints from us [meaning from Christians].' He confessed, 'It doesn't always work. But you have to try to look at the good side of things.' Debby, seventeen, felt that for her work now came second. 'God is the priority. And so it seems to come easier with less worry.'

Five girls and two boys said being a Christian made no difference to work, but many, and proportionately more boys than girls, said they tried much harder now. Two girls felt they were less grudging about work since they had become Christians, and two others valued money and material rewards less than before. Many said that prayer helped relieve the tensions of work, and a few said that Bible study had the same effect. Five felt that their faith made it necessary for them to choose what sort of work to do, rather than simply doing whatever became available. They stated that they had no intention now of doing what they called 'unchristian' work, meaning work that compromised Christian standards.

The future

Does being a Christian make a difference to the way you approach the future? In answer to this question, most said they were trusting God to lead them, or even that 'it's up to God now'. Many also felt that their own attitude to the future had become more constructive and positive. Paul told us, 'It's given me more excitement about life in the future.' Melanie, a former glue-sniffer, said, 'It's made a big difference, because I never thought I had a future. I'd never look to next week or even tomorrow 'cos I was so scared of what it held for me.' David, with great satisfaction, replied, 'Well, I know I'm going somewhere for some reason, but as yet I don't know what.'

Claire stated, 'It's not in your hands any more,' and Derek nodded decisively as he said, 'If I go my own way, it'll not work out.' Alan explained, 'Well, I'd like to think—it doesn't work out that way always—that I try and see if this is God's plan for me or not, before jumping in at the deep end.' As an example, he said he had prayed about which 'O' levels he should take, was content with the answer he said he had received, and had acted accordingly.

Barry's answer was brief, blunt and perceptive. 'I see it as not being easy. I see it as we'll grow.' But Graham was more enthusiastic. 'Whereas before I was just plodding along in the same old rut, getting deeper and deeper, now every corner's a different avenue. I cannot explain it. It's just everything's different. I can't put a word to it apart from "fantastic".' Barbara's reply more or less covered both these points. She believed, 'Being a Christian helps you to be positive, 'cos you realize that even though you are going to come up to hard times, there's always something better ahead which will help you.'

In their replies, many referred to the fact that they were no longer scared of dying. As one put it, 'You know you're going somewhere because there's life after death.' This knowledge, they said, gave them a greater assurance. In relation to this aspect of the future, fifteen-year-old Alison gave us the most unusual answer when she said, 'I'm always thinking about the second coming. What that does is it stops me putting things off.' Nevertheless, nine of the people we questioned did not think that being a Christian made any difference to their approach to the future, or at least they were not sure that it did.

Life in general

So did being a Christian make any difference to life in general? Most of the young people we interviewed seemed to be looking on the bright side. They also felt that they now saw things differently from non-believers. Many said that they found life much more worthwhile and purposeful now. As one boy put it, in words we heard several times, 'Before I was a Christian I didn't really think there was any purpose in life. I thought 'ife just went on.' Nearly half of those who answered this question, most of them girls, spoke of having a more relaxed approach to life, while some of the boys emphasized the joy that life now held for them. 'For me, life has brought joy and happiness and lots of friends,' declared Paul. Ruth stated, 'You feel different and notice different things. God made it all and it's beautiful.'

'Now I've got something to live for,' said Laura. Sharon agreed, saying 'You're not just here to live a normal, everyday life. I don't know how to put this really, but there's more to life than living.' Tracy put it this way: 'It's meant that I know there is always someone I can rely on, and it's not just all work, exams, a job, marriage and a family.' Wendy's explanation was this: 'More than anything you realize that you don't have to face life alone. It gives you an optimistic outlook.'

One boy said he found life in general harder now, because

he had to endure much criticism. Four of those questioned did not know whether it had made a difference or not, though several girls and one boy believed that their faith had given them more understanding about life than they'd had before. Emma made this comment:

'I've got a peace now. You sort of know where you're going, and you don't know what's happening the next day but you know, whatever it is, it's right. I try to make a point every morning of saying, "Lord, I give this day to you."'

One last individual comment is perhaps worth recording, from sixteen-year-old Rebecca. The difference for her was this:

'Yes, I think it's more upsetting, when you're a Christian, to look around the world and see what's going on than it was when you weren't. Then you just thought everything was all right and nothing was worrying or bothering. Nothing needed putting right. But now you can see that the world's in chaos.'

Problems

Chapter 10 explores many of the problems that the young people acknowledged they faced as Christians. They were asked if being a Christian made a difference to problems and to the way they approached them. Apart from one boy who said he did not know, they all confirmed that their approach to problems had altered markedly. By far the most common answer stressed the need for and the value of prayer. As Sara reminded us, 'My weapon, my protection, is prayer.' 'I always ask God to help, and he does,' affirmed Ed. Again and again we were told that God helps, reassures in a crisis, and 'brings you through'. Anne's explanation ran like this:

'Yes, I'll often struggle with something and it will take a long time before I bring it before God. Usually it's that way round. But I know that God can handle my problems. There's no problem that's too hard for him. And if I take it to him, he'll deal with it. He'll help me out with it.'

Pat made her point rather differently:

22

'I'm not very good at sorting problems out. I just tend to leave them—sort of try and leave them to sort themselves out... I won't sit and keep praying and saying, "Please help me with this, that and the other." I just tend to sit down and say, "Well I can't do anything about this so you'll have to do something about it." It's a case of being aware of the fact that I can't sort it out and that to try to will probably make a bigger mess. It's difficult. It's sort of like a case of thinking, when you can't swim and you jump into a pool, it's going to be OK because somebody's going to drag me out... It's dead hard, but that's the only way I can do it.'

Bottling up or trying to repress problems is never healthy, and we were impressed by many teenagers who said they were prepared now to share their problems with other Christians, and also talk them through. Louise's answer is typical:

'Before, I would just have sat and suffered and so it would have got worse, and I'd have gone to school friends for advice and they would be going through the same problems and they couldn't help themselves either. But talking to Christian friends at church has helped because they've been through it too. And going through it as a Christian and going through it as a non-Christian, well, there are different ways somehow. I think it's harder going through it as a Christian because you know what you should be like, and God says you've got to be like Jesus, haven't you? Sometimes I pray with faith this big (she showed a tiny division on a ruler), but a lot has changed in my own personality and next time I'm facing the same sort of problem, it's easier to cope with.'

Several others said that coping with problems was harder because their Christian standards were higher than those they had previously lived by. Tim said, 'Now I've got a lot more—I've had to give up my favourite music, and also my non-Christian girl-friends.' Yet he would agree with Keith, who said that his faith 'sort of helps me cope with different and difficult situations'. John said he tried to handle his problems by trying to remember something in the Bible which talked about the thing which he was doing:

'If so, I'll try and do what the Bible says about it, but if I can't think of something from the Bible, I sort of think, well what would he [i.e. Jesus] do standing here faced with this problem? And I think like that is the best way. Not what would my friends do, but what would he do?'

And Richard told us his faith gave him more strength just to cope with life:

'I still feel that life kicks you in the teeth and that. I can't understand how people can survive without Christ.'

Attitude to others

Only three young people felt that their attitude to others was no different. All the rest said very specifically that their approach had altered, often quite dramatically. Most said that they were much more patient and caring, and more understanding and tolerant. Conversely, they felt they were less critical, bitchy and suspicious. What they told us certainly suggested that their attitudes were more responsible and considerate. One girl admitted to angry feelings:

'I could quite easily smack some people in the mouth. I stand there and I say to myself, No, I'm a Christian, so I shouldn't. But I'd really like to plant them one in the mouth, and I have to keep saying to myself, No, I cannot hit you because I love you.'

And one of the boys made this remark:

'Strange as it is, I just haven't got it in me to hate people, even if they're rotten to me.'

Peter was trying to improve his attitudes:

'I try to see them as the Lord sees them. I try not to despise anyone. Sometimes that's easy and sometimes that's hard.'

David was trying to keep some contact with his former friends. This led him to make the following comment:

'Well sometimes you go back to your old bunch of friends and you think, "Well, this lot are disgusting." You know, you don't understand the way they are, and you have to think, "Well, I was like that once," so in a way you've got to sympathize with

24

them. You do look at them differently. But I can only get so close to them and I can't get any further, 'cos I realize that what they do is not the same as what I do.'

Other comments were that they listened more to others, and were more sensitive towards them, trying to love them and to get on with them, and not be offensive to them. Also, they were becoming more careful in what they said to others. Stuart said: 'I'm a lot sort of calmer with people. I don't fly off the handle with them. I accept people as they are.' Tricia's method was, 'If a person's narking me, I just think, "Come on Lord, you've got to help me," and I soon calm down again.'

Wayne agreed that being a Christian changed the way you look at people, to some extent at least:

'I mean, you can't help just liking some people, 'cos that's human nature, whether you're a Christian or not. But you tend to accept more people now. I mean you give them more of a chance to like them.'

And Mary assured us:

'It's helped me to talk to people I'd never have talked to before. And it's surprising. Some of the people you decide you dislike, and then when you pray about it, you realize they're not so bad as you thought they were.'

Attitude to self

Last, we asked them whether their view of themselves had changed because of their Christian commitment. Eight of the teenagers said they were not sure about this, but all the others believed there was some difference, at least. Alan admitted that his attitude fluctuated with time and how he was feeling:

'When I'm on a spiritual high, I see myself as a servant of God, and then when I'm not on a spiritual high, I tend to see myself as a hindrance to a heavenly scheme, and the benefits aren't coming through.'

Brenda would have agreed with that assessment:

'It shows me I'm not perfect, that I've got a lot of faults in me.

25

But it helps me to learn from them and so try to build a better person.'

Before she became a Christian, Melanie had no regard for herself whatsoever:

'It's hard to think of myself any different to what I did before—which wasn't very much. But there are times when I do think of myself as something to be valued. I do think that deep down, but it's my head that's been filled with rubbish. Everyone else used to say I was a drunk and I wasn't worth the bother.'

Although from a very different background, Laura felt similarly: 'Sometimes you feel, "Oh I'm a nobody."' Where Melanie was helped to think more positively about herself by faithful Christian friends, Laura found her encouragement from the Bible:

'You read things in the Bible and they help you through things like that, and then you begin to see, "Oh well, I am important to God even though a lot of people may not think me important at all."'

In marked contrast, Graham stated, 'I'm just a different person. I'm happier. I'm more content with myself.' And Beth told us:

'I see myself as special now, because I know he loves me, and because I know I am important to somebody—him. Now I can be myself, and be confident and useful.'

This is a particularly important observation, and one which few other people mentioned. This is hardly surprising, since it usually takes time for Christians to realize that one result of the transformation gradually taking place in them is that they are able to be themselves, the selves they were created to be. Eighteen-year-old John was certainly becoming aware of this:

'Before, I wasn't pleased with myself because the way I saw things was that everyone else was better. But since I took the step, I have found that over the six years I have been able to be myself. I mean, if you don't, how can you love your mother or your father?'

The difference for Colin was that 'now I expect more of

myself than I expect of other people'. Derek put a particular gloss on this kind of remark. He agreed that his view of himself was no longer anything like it had been, saying, 'Yes, I know I'm totally helpless whereas before I thought I could do anything.' Probably at the back of his mind he was recalling the warning of Jesus to his disciples that 'without me you can do nothing'.

We end this section with some honest words of Jane, a seventeen-year-old from Wales, because they underline the struggle so many of these young people—in common with Christians of all ages everywhere—are involved in, in relation to self. Yes, she did see herself differently now:

'Obviously I know all the bad points now. I'm constantly aware of that. All the things I do wrongly, you know. And how I still see my old self coming through, which is a killer, and sometimes I'm stubborn as well. I can be stubborn not to let go of my old self, and I'll see it happening and I'll start enjoying it. Because I'm stubborn I think, "No, I want to enjoy myself." And yet, if I'd let my self go, I would enjoy myself more.'

Jane's answer is typical of the frank and open replies we were privileged to receive from almost all the young people. They were absolutely clear that their Christian commitment had made real differences in their lives and outlook. While many stressed that it was hard for them to live up to the Christian standards they had espoused, what comes through their answers is a real determination to try to live for God, to please him, and to be better with others.

Most of them now claimed to have a new assurance and confidence, new hope, happiness, and peace. Their changing outlook was providing them with new expectations about themselves and their lives. And they showed a refreshing readiness to pray, to ask advice, and to share their feelings and problems. Naivety and ingenuousness were inevitably still present in many things they said and thought. But their pleasure in their faith, and their desire to grow and develop as Christians were also obvious.

3
A Living God

I don't think he sits up there on a cloud, you know. I think he's like a part of us. I suppose he must put up with a lot.

Love. That means that whatever I've done, no matter which road I take, I can always come back to him.

In this chapter we want to consider how the young people we interviewed thought about God. 'Theology' is an attempt to think clearly about the various affirmations of religion by which one lives—it is 'faith seeking understanding'. It also entails trying to be consistent, at least as far as that is possible when there are paradoxes. Many of our experiences do not fit tidily into pre-set categories. Often we talk about God only as an alternative to being reduced to silence. How did these teenagers fare?

To ask what somebody believes about God is fraught with problems, of course. We hoped to find out a little about the ideas of God the young people were working with, whetherthere was a 'creed within a creed', how far they gave evidence of serious thought and what was omitted or seldom mentioned.

One way into a person's working theology is to ask about images or pictures. Images imply concepts and doctrines; they may also point out areas of tension and confusion.

Images of God

Six of those interviewed felt the need to deny that God was 'a person', by which they meant a human being or in human form. However, one of them was still engaged in a debate about whether God had arms and legs. Did the 'image of God' mean God was in the image of a human being? The young man in question inclined to the view that it did not but the fact that the debate could be taken seriously indicated that some very knowledgeable young people could still operate at a very naive level.

Others accepted conventional images while realizing that they were no more than picture language and not to be taken literally. God was 'an old man with a white beard', he had 'long hair' ('the influence of TV'), 'long knees and huge hands', he was 'a massive sort of thing with a beard', 'dark with a white robe', he was 'a huge hand with a person kneeling on it'. It is difficult to know how seriously to take these responses. After all, what do you say when a total stranger asks you this kind of thing out of the blue? We had to accept, as Tim observed, that most images would be 'influenced by pictures, drawings, stained glass windows or whatever'.

Some responses were more idiosyncratic and less conventional. They were reactions against the anthropo-morphisms and tried to capture a sense of mystery and infinity. God is a 'mist', a 'cloud', a 'force' ('but you can't say, "Hey, force!"'), 'light', 'a room filled with white light', 'a great white being', 'a head surrounded with light', 'everything is perfect...sort of white and glowing', 'rolling flames'. These pictures represented an attempt to reflect an intensity of experience.

Others turned to images of care and love. God is 'a bundle of love', 'benign with a silk gown', 'a tender face', 'a shoulder to cry on'. The language of relationships makes the same point. God is 'uncle', 'big brother', 'an old man who I treat like a granddad', 'a kindly old man with love for his children'.

Two young people mentioned spatial images:

'I sort of picture him right at the top. And Jesus below him. And the Spirit's below him. I'm not on about status. That's just the way I see them. Father, Son, and Holy Spirit.'

'I think that he's right up above us so that sometimes when I

pray or try to think of God I actually look up. I kind of look up...
It's just that he's there.'

For eleven out of the total number, trying to picture God was unproductive. They preferred to think of a sense of presence. So Beth said, 'When I'm in the countryside I can feel the wind and the power.' Laura also had no picture but still said, 'I sort of sense him.' For Alan, this sense was particularly strong:

'I have had a few tries to deny God exists, an anti-God feeling when I've been thinking of plays where the religion is just out of fear, and I've found it completely impossible because I know perfectly well that God is actually there...it's a personal presence.'

The idea of a presence shaded off into the notion that God was everywhere and in everyone. However incoherent Tom's thoughts might be, they represented a personal wrestling with this concept:

'I don't like the way people think of God as a person on a throne. You know—with guardian angels, and him on the throne, and we all look up to him. I can't come to terms with that... I consider God as a sort of force, you know. You can look at it that way. It's something that's in all of us. Maybe when we die, for instance, it's not someone we go and see when we die but he's sort of with us now, maybe our emotions and our feelings. You know, he may be the good side of you. And, like, the devil as the sort of evil side of you. You know the theory about this big explosion...and this big explosion is God. Well, I might accept the fact that it might be true, but the actual thing of calling it God, I do not accept, because I don't think I should be worshipping some big explosion sort of thing. So I think I'd rather, in the sense of worship, worship something that is good, but something that is in all of us, our emotions, our feelings, something that is a backbone for everybody.'

Wayne covered much the same ground but picked out an unusual implication of this view:

'I don't think he sits up there on a cloud, you know. I think he's like a part of us. I suppose he must put up with a lot.'

30

An invitation to talk about images of God is bound to lead some into trinitarian models, the idea of God as three-in-one, Father, Son and Holy Spirit. Twelve replies focused on the doctrine, and seven others showed that the people concerned were thinking hard about the idea that Jesus Christ was God. Four of these people saw the Trinity as a problem which needed to be thought about. The rest revealed a moderate amount of confusion, the sense that this language was saying something important about God and a good deal of honest struggle and reflection.

For example, Keith remembered his Sunday School teacher:

'I was taught once that you can be a few things; you can be a father and a son and a brother and an uncle and a nephew and so that's how I try to explain it. That's what I try to explain to my dad and I don't think he listens half the time.'

Nick drew on his reading of the classic children's fantasy books by C.S. Lewis about the land of Narnia, in which a mighty lion called Aslan is sometimes seen as a God-like figure:

'When people mention God I think of the whole Trinity. The best definition I can think of...well, I read a book, a commentary in C.S. Lewis' books, and it went back to one bit where a boy asked Aslan, who's a personification of God and Jesus, who he was. And the lion said, "Myself," in a deep and mighty voice— that was God's. Then he said, "Myself," again in a happier voice—and that was Jesus. And he said, "Myself," in a fleeting voice, a spiritual voice, and that was the Holy Spirit. And that's how I see them really—as a mighty presence, a happy person and a fleeting person, all in one.'

Pat is in another league. She is a thoughtful Catholic, beginning to work through what she has received to a personal appropriation and understanding of the tradition:

'Sometimes I'll see God in a light of this father face and I'll feel that I need the sort of protective father figure and that's what I pray to, the father aspect of God. Sometimes I'll see it as a friend and brother I need. A younger person type of thing and

31

then it'll be a Jesus type prayer. And then sometimes I feel that I just need to feel the Spirit. For me there's different personalities of God and I still see it all as God. But ultimately I would say that the Jesus aspect and the Spirit aspect were just aspects of God. The main thing I see God as is a big thing, sort of an engulfing God, and whatever that is I see it as. I don't see it as formless. It's like...a sort of a thought. There seems a big thought who thinks... It feels infinite because it's sort of got these big arms round the world.'

Attributes of God

Not surprisingly the majority of responses picked out the love of God as the central characteristic. Forty-one of the sixty-seven we interviewed mentioned this quality: God is 'Father', 'loving', 'like my Dad', who loves so much 'it sends shivers down my spine'. Debby said she could almost feel 'the arm round your shoulders'. For Heather, God is 'a parent, who will sit and listen and understand' (and perhaps most importantly) 'who won't contradict you. He gives you freedom to speak.' He is 'the perfect friend who is there all the time', 'open-armed', 'someone who takes the bad bits and makes them not matter'. It is impossible to do justice to the range of comments, but one or two may give some idea of the strength of feeling expressed by many of these young Christians:

'Love. That means that whatever I've done, no matter which road I take, I can always come back to him.'

'We hurt him terribly, yet he still cares for us... We're left to go our own way and so in consequence we often do things which really must hurt him very much, yet he's always ready to welcome us back.'

'God is love. And I really believe that. I don't believe at all in the judgmental nature of God...this thing about God judging in the end. I don't believe that at all. I just believe in the positive, in the love, the creative force we choose to call God... It created me in the beginning and watches me grow up like watching a child

walk, taking the first steps and knowing that it is going to fall over and that it will probably hurt itself but knowing that it's got to learn to walk.'

A substantial number, eighteen of the sixty-seven, mentioned power as a key attribute of God. This was expressed in different ways: 'He's the central point.' At the end of time, 'Satan will be kicked into the lake of fire.' God must be powerful 'to resurrect Jesus'. 'If it wasn't for him, I wouldn't be here.' 'I think of power and anger in a way.'

'He is almighty and he's all powerful. He created the world. I mean sometimes I forget just how powerful he is.'

'I think of him as mighty first, who you should really fear, and all powerful.'

'He is strong, but evil is strong as well. I believe evil and God fight each other. There is a continuous battle going on everywhere under everyone and outside... God will triumph over evil eventually. He's bound to. I don't honestly know why, but I believe that myself. I've read it, and people have told us good will triumph over evil. At one time I said, "Oh no, no way. There's so much evil." But I think eventually good will overcome and evil be banished.'

These comments are soundly orthodox, and in the above comment one young man, Ed, was partly responding to what he had been told about God's omnipotence. John had come to his conviction that God was powerful by a different route. From the age of four he had been afflicted with a terrible stutter. The fear of speaking in public still remained but he told us that, though not completely healed, he was being healed. Out of his personal experience came his conviction about the power of God:

'Some people think that God is a different God now to what he was then, that he's not so powerful now. But the fact is that he's the same God now that he's always been. He's exactly the same. He's just as powerful. We seem to think that Satan has got an awful lot of power...but the fact is that God is the most powerful. He's Lord of Lords.'

Linked to the power of God was the sense that that power

was personally directed towards our good in providential care and protection. It was here that general beliefs about God's love and power were earthed. God cares about the smallest details of our lives and arranges events so that they come out to a good end. Nineteen of those questioned fastened upon some evidence that God was personally active in what had happened to them:

'I went to a course in London…and I hadn't made any conscious choice about going but everything just flowed along… I think God was really working through other people to make sure I got there.'

Derek was confused about whether he should go into the RAF. He handed the problem over to God. A possible job came up but the interview was over in five minutes. His interpretation is interesting:

'God overruled… I gave him the problem.'

Ed wanted to be a pilot and failed his medical:

'Those few words shattered my life. He absolutely didn't want me to be a pilot. It's as simple as that.'

Later he could say:

'The Lord got me a job… He just put it on my heart…soon as I saw it at the Job Centre. Interviewed twelve people. Me and this other lad got the job.'

Tracy found that the knowledge of God's providence helped her face the possibility of failure:

'I think God knows where he wants me to be, and whatever happens, he'll be there, and even if I make a muck-up of it, sort of, he'll be there to sort it out. If I didn't pass my 'A' levels at the right grade, I would interpret that as meaning that God didn't want me to go to university.'

In a more dramatic vein, John told us of an occasion when a gang of youths was waiting for him and some friends:

'When we walked out they were all standing there, so I said, "Right Lord, put your angels between us and them and don't let them get through." And we just walked past them, you know.'

For Sara, this belief transformed her wish to follow a particular career into a vocation and a divine call:

'I feel I've been directed towards working with handicapped children. I think that's what God wants me to do.'

The belief in God's care applied to all kinds of situation. Sometimes the problem seemed trivial in the extreme—a matter of a parking space:

'I only passed my test in March and I am still a bit nervous going into a multi-storey, as you hold everyone else up. I just sat there in the queue and said, "Lord, find me a space." And he did, you know. One on the second floor and I wasn't holding anybody up.'

But sometimes it is literally a matter of life and death. Melanie had experienced serious drug addiction and alcoholism. She spoke about a Christian who had been her lifeline:

'The thing that's kept me in it and determined to go on is X. I only met her about six months ago. I believe that this friendship—I know it sounds daft—is from God in a way. She's given me... I feel a bit funny saying this—more love in them six months than I've ever had in my life.'

Here of all places we felt that their theology touched bedrock. Beliefs about God's power and care give them a perspective by which to interpret their lives. At its worst it may smack of fatalism—'whatever will be will be', or idleness—'I need not work, think, prepare, revise...because God will see me through.' At its best such convictions can produce a sense of vocation or an attitude which transforms disaster. As Tim put it:

'Everything God does has a time. I realize myself that my timing doesn't coincide with his but that he does what is best for me, however it may seem at the time.'

The active acceptance of the will of God and an unshakeable belief in his goodness, 'though the mountains crumble', are both profoundly Biblical responses.

Tim's comment suggests an important corrective to any tendency we might have to interpret all this as basically consumerist. It is true that God is personal and involved with their problems but he is not necessarily 'on tap' to provide anything they want when they want it. Twenty-eight mentioned the severity of God, twelve of whom had already spoken of God's love. We thought this was a surprisingly large number. Taken together they depict a God who is 'hard', a 'hound of heaven', driving and testing, chastening and disciplining, even allowing unpleasant things to happen, but, of course, only for one's ultimate good.

Some of their comments communicated the flavour of this position:

'Sometimes he's hard on you.' 'It's as though God was shaking me.' 'I was scared he'd take away my ballet.' 'The cushy way isn't the way he wants us to go.' 'Sometimes he gives me a clip round the ear.' 'He is constantly hard—he tests us all the time.' 'I do feel that sometimes he sort of pulls me up and says, "Now what the hell do you think you're doing?"' 'It might be his will if I fail my exams.' 'He can be hard on people; I mean he can put you through a lot of problems.' 'He's always pushing you to the limit.'

Few suggested that the 'hard time' was the result of pique or capriciousness on God's part. One girl explained her sister's serious illness as 'God testing us all'. She continued:

'Well, maybe God wants to teach us something through this. I mean it's his will as to what's going to happen to her in the end, but it's proving hard for Mum and Dad and I sometimes think it's unfair... There was a time when I felt that he was punishing me for something. But I've grown out of that and I believe that he's trying us... I don't think I feel as bitter as I used to... Sometimes I may think he's harsh and cruel but no, he's not. He's not really.'

This mature response to the difficulties of faith in the presence of suffering, like those already mentioned, has to be set against some of the easy, slightly thoughtless comments which we have included in the chapter on prayer. There is no uniform picture. A substantial number did not see God as a slot machine, obediently responding to every whim and demand. They had room in their theology for God as a being who refines the individual's character through fiery trials.

The omissions

The full impact of these responses was only felt when we asked ourselves what was missing. It seemed to us that two aspects of God's nature were absent from most of the replies.

The first concerned the concept of God's majesty. This feature includes ideas such as the sense of awe and mystery, the shudder in the soul and dread in the presence of something that cannot be described. Very few young people picked up this aspect of God. In fact, we were unable to find more than three definite instances.

Wendy just about qualified:

'I just imagine this very holy Father, holy presence, very awesome being...definitely a really almighty power.'

Jill was asked about beliefs which were significant for her, which 'really came alive'. She replied in this way:

'I think knowing God's so high and mighty. He's totally powerful and I'm so small and weak and one of thousands of millions , but he still loves me.'

Mike probably came closest to the concept of majesty:

'He is almighty and he's all powerful. He created the world. He is also a king and all powerful and so quite often I come into his presence, you know, and say, "Thank you Lord for doing this." It's really great and I just remember that he's Lord of the universe... It's important to remember that he is the majesty and you've got to remember his majesty when you come into his presence.'

These examples are not especially reminiscent of Isaiah's 'Holy, holy, holy' or Moses' dread before the burning bush. Put another way, the young people found it easier to think of God as father than as a mighty king.

The second omission concerned the size of God. We have already seen that God is loving, powerful, demanding yet intimately concerned with the details of one's life. These young Christians seldom seemed to take account in their thinking of a God big enough to be involved in the government of the world, let alone the universe. This was the other side of the personalizing, even privatizing, of the divine activity. His undoubted powers tended to be exercised within the immediate circle of the individual's concerns. The cosmic was reduced to the individual. The existentialist element was predominant in their theology.

Problems relating to God

There were three problem areas which had to do with the understanding of God and which were mentioned sufficiently often to warrant comment.

The first was the fact that he is invisible. This was hardly surprising since many adult Christians would point to the same difficulty. Why can't God be more like other people?

'I think the most difficult thing really is that you can't see him. You can't actually see something visual. He manifests himself, you know, in healings and things like that and you know there's someone there but you can't actually see him. That is quite hard... I do doubt him a lot of times but never seriously.'

'I find it difficult that God is not here as a person to talk to, say like you and me, and that he is invisible. Yes, around, but not here as a person. That is difficult for me because if a person is sitting in a room it is easy to talk to them...'

'The biggest thing is not being able to have a conversation with him half the time. It seems to be only one way most of the time, because you're talking and he's not saying a lot.'

The second problem was that of suffering. Obviously any theology which failed to see suffering as a problem in the light of the doctrine of God's love would be inadequate. We thought most of the young people would deal with this issue. In fact it was not discussed as often as we would have expected, though twenty-two did recognize suffering as a question requiring some kind of answer.

At one end we would locate Carol's rather unreflective comment:

'Natural disasters are God's way of saying there are too

38

many people. Is this cruel? Maybe.'

Others more thoughtfully came up with a version of the free-will defence. Derek's answer was one of the most coherent and passionate:

'Why does God allow such and such, like an evil person like Idi Amin? I used to find that hard to answer. Why is there evil? Why if God's so fantastic did he have to make us with a flaw? Right and wrong... I find that difficult but we're in that position because he's given us a free choice. That's fantastic that someone like that's given us a free choice to say, "I don't believe in this or that," when he could go (clicks his fingers) just like that and you'll want it or he'll finish you right there. He just sits and takes all the abuse and sees people suffering for him when he could have had a perfect world if he'd wanted.'

And there were a few for whom the problem could not remain academic. In the tradition of the psalms of lament they accused God, even from within the standpoint of faith. Some of these responses were among the most moving we encountered:

'How can God let me go through the life that I've led and now expect me to think, "Praise God"? I find that hard and I can't understand why. I remember writing a letter to somebody before I became a Christian and I put in it that I have tried praying, and I prayed for my family not to be separated but now Mum and Dad are divorced and is this what God deals in, splitting families?'

Another big issue was that of science and faith. This well-worked theme refuses to lie down, despite the voluminous literature on the subject. Whether old conflicts have been resolved or not, no one can ignore the effect of popular science or 'scientism' on faith. The scientific culture produces a climate of opinion in which thinking responsibly about God becomes extremely difficult. This partly explains why Elaine fastened on the debate about the Turin Shroud. It offered a possible way of defending the resurrection in terms a scientist would accept. 'You know it's true inside. But proofs for your friends are difficult.' We wonder what she

39

will do now that the Shroud has been shown to be a medieval product.

Often the teenagers who studied science saw the issue as a potential source of tension. Ed commented:

'Physics and geography are two sciences which contradict a lot of what the Bible says. Although I believe the Bible, I should really go against everything I've been taught at school but I don't. Like I said about Genesis, the world's changed. We know about atoms, molecules, electrons, radiation and all that sort of thing in Physics, so it's hard for us to be both. I think I've got a happy compromise between them.'

For Colin, the happy compromise consisted in separating faith and science into watertight compartments:

'I have a scientific mind. I keep science and religion apart.'

No one had any doctrine of God the creator which would encompass the science they studied at school. Whatever line they took personally, a substantial number saw the creation-evolution debate as an either-or. Miracles were to be swallowed uncritically or rejected firmly. Continuous creation did not figure in their thinking. They seemed to have done no philosophy of religion in the classroom or Christian apologetics in the church. We could find next to no evidence of any systematic study of the worlds and languages of science and faith. Our inquiries suggested that, though their faith is often vibrant, and their sense of God's presence deeply felt and genuine, their thinking about God, perhaps not surprisingly, lacks sophistication.

4

A Personal Saviour

He's one of the lads, you know. He's not like one of them with cupped hands going around drinking chocolate.

He was a Jewish person and he spoke Jewish and he acted Jewish.

He's blasted away the barrier of sin between us and God.

But we are here to live our lives for God...by the pattern Jesus showed us.

In the course of our interviews we asked two basic questions about Christ. The first gave young people the opportunity to pick out any aspect of his nature and attributes which they thought important. The second required them to explain why they thought Christ was special and why he held a central place in Christianity. We hoped that these questions would correspond roughly to the traditional distinction between the person and work of Christ.

In the event things were nothing like so tidy. The young people's comments did not fit into the categories we had set up for them. As a result, we had to find a new way to organize our findings. Moreover, they often mentioned Jesus throughout the interview even in areas which on the surface were concerned with other issues. We might well have anticipated this and, undoubtedly, it provided us with a wealth of personal data, all the more useful because it was volunteered unselfconsciously.

Such a range and variety of response made analysis

difficult. In the end we found ourselves listening for those themes which seemed to 'come alive' for a substantial number. In our view, five figure prominently enough to justify their being amalgamated to form 'the Christ of young Christians'.

Before examining these five themes it is as well to deal with the question of their orthodoxy. Previous research has often commented on the fact that most young Christians happily associate themselves with traditional doctrinal formulations. Leslie Francis, for example, in his study has said that 87 per cent of teenagers seem content to accept the notion that Jesus is the Son of God. A third of our sample mentioned the divinity of Jesus, even though they were not asked the question directly. Their replies were often the preamble to a longer statement dealing with some aspect of Christ's person with which they were deeply concerned. This meant that sometimes the impeccably sound reply gave the impression of being a nod in the direction of orthodoxy rather than a heartfelt conviction. They accepted the belief as part of the Christian package; they had not yet made it their own:

'Jesus is God and part of God.' 'He is definitely one with God.' 'You can't separate Jesus and God.' 'He's the same as God.' 'He's the same as God, a sort of God.' 'He is God in human form.' 'I think of God and Jesus as perfect.' 'He is the Son of God.'

Only three of those who mentioned the subject seemed to have difficulties. Linda saw Christ as the perfect Christian:

'If I had to describe Jesus I'd probably say that he'd...was the sort of... Well, I'd say that he was God's son but that I find it difficult. I'd probably say he was somebody who spoke...brought God's message to us, to earth, who was perfect...well, all that he was teaching... He was a perfect person, a perfect Christian who we could never really copy but who we should try and be like.'

Characteristically, Pat was developing her own position:

'I don't understand how he could be God made man. But it's important to me that he is. And that he was a man with a man's

confusion. And I believe that he really didn't know all along that he was God.'

As we have already indicated, we often felt that the orthodox comments lacked something. When they spoke of other aspects of the person of Christ the teenagers began to communicate conviction rather than assent. Each of the five themes which we will now discuss represents a substantial cluster of replies. It is our contention that a majority of young Christians share these perspectives on Christ.

A real human being

The first attribute to note is their insistence on Jesus' humanity. Thirty out of sixty-seven wanted to make the point that Jesus was a real human being. They emphasized his earthly appearance, stressing his Jewishness, his ordinariness, his youthfulness, his endurance of pain and his strength. Sometimes the picture came close to the Jesus of the film producer Zeffirelli; occasionally it reflected the traditions of Christian art. But the basic message was that Jesus was a strong, heroic, modern sort of person; he was emphatically not boring.

Jesus was described as 'a younger man', a little 'like a Renaissance painting', 'an ordinary person', 'a man you would trust'. He is a 'big bloke', 'an outward bloke', just 'a normal Jewish fellow who oozes peace'. 'His eyes would be nice', and he was probably 'dark, with a Jew's nose'.

'I like to dwell on when he was getting baptized and the dove hit him.'

'He's one of the lads, you know. He's not like one of them with cupped hands going around drinking chocolate. He's one of the lads.'

The attractiveness of the humanity of Christ was asserted by Tom despite his problems with some of the traditional elements in the faith—miracles, the virgin birth, the resurrection and the idea of God as Father, Son and Spirit—the Trinity:

'He was a Jewish person and he spoke Jewish and he acted Jewish and it's a funny thing, you know, but when people say, "I can't imagine Jesus going on television," and things like that, just because he's Jesus, I think maybe we should understand more that he was human. And he did do human things just as we do human things... His basic constituency, if you'd like to call it that, is that he was human. Even down to drinking wine, going to the toilet, getting up and sleeping and things like that.'

What is significant about these comments is the way in which they reflect the pressures on the teenage Christian. They can be construed as an attempt to counter the widespread assumption that to be a Christian is just not part of the image of a normal, healthy, fun-loving teenager. They pick up the anxiety that Jesus might be seen as wet or wimpish. This fear accounts for the stress on his strength and his normality. Their portrait of Christ is partly a reaction to their peers' estimate of religion.

A true friend

Twenty-eight replies stressed a different aspect of Christ's person. For these young people Jesus was a constant friend and companion. He was always with them, instantly available, and he had promised that he would never leave them. He was the perfect friend, counsellor and confidant. They could unburden themselves to Christ without fear of rebuff:

'I think of him as a helper. He seems to walk alongside you.'

'An extra friend. It's what people frequently say to me... I've had an awful day and how do I still manage to keep a grin on my face? They say, "Why?" and I say, "I've got an extra friend who's always with me, who I can always turn to." He's always pleasant to be with.'

'I'm not the most intelligent person in the world, in fact, I'm not most things, but he loves me for what I am. He doesn't push us around, you know.'

'He's not like so-called friends who run away and desert you when things go wrong. He's always there and he can give you the

44

love that you need and all the attention and care that you need as well.'

'I can be driving around in the car, without a radio sometimes too, and without being a Christian I'd probably feel very lonely. But I know the Lord's with me and when I'm down I know he's still there with me. He doesn't say, "I'll come back to you when you're in a better mood."'

The picture of Christ as one who is pleasant to be with, good company, able to give you care and attention, someone who does not push you around and is unperturbed by mood swings is an identikit of the perfect companion, the ideal which no school friend can ever approach. Some seem to go even further in the direction of intimacy. Jesus is pre-eminently the listener, one who shares all your secrets, supportive and non-directive, a mixture of perfect counsellor and agony aunt:

'Your friends don't always understand you and you don't understand your friends. But he'll always listen to you. Sometimes your friends don't want to listen to you. No one wants to listen to what you've got to say. But he always listens and he'll always be there and can offer you love and a listening ear.'

'I just think of him as an ordinary person. He's very willing to listen to people.'

'If you want somebody to talk to, you turn to Jesus like, say, as a friend... He's somebody who you discuss things with and sometimes you can even ask opinions.'

'I think Jesus is for the younger person and he allows you to change what you're thinking. You know, you can have your own opinions.'

When friends are unkind and parents nag, Jesus will listen and understand. Perhaps the key to this view of Christ is once again to be found in the nature of adolescence. The teenage years are a period when you are often unsure of your welcome. Christ is totally accepting. He represents a safe place in a bruising world. He is, after all, 'for the younger person' and 'allows you to have your own opinions'.

45

One who knows

Jesus has been through it all. In the style of the letter to the Hebrews these teenagers wanted to signal that Jesus had been 'tested in every way as we are'. About a fifth of them identified their own sufferings with those of Christ. They often added that, as a result, 'you can relate to him'; 'he makes it easier to bear'; 'he's been through everything'; 'he knows what it's like'. The experiences of Christ make it possible for the teenager to bear ridicule or cope with despair:

'He suffered as a person. That makes you feel better, doesn't it? 'Cos you know that he's been tempted and you know what he feels like... He knows what the friction in life is and the ups and downs and to be deserted and lonely. He must have been lonely millions of times. Well, his disciples, all they were thinking of were going out to bury their dead father or they had to go home and say hello to their wives.'

'I prefer to think of him as the man, because it is more important to me to know that he got depressed, that he got let down by his friends, to know that he was angry. Things like "Jesus didn't lose his temper because he was perfect", well, Jesus must have felt really, really angry inside. And to know that when I feel that come on, it's all right to feel like that.'

This kind of comment is significant because it seems to us to be another point at which the doctrine of Christ touches adolescent experience. Not every interpersonal encounter makes teenagers feel good about themselves. On the contrary, there are many negative views about teenagers that young people are likely to encounter. They not uncommonly experience rejection from parents and peers, even if this is usually short-lived. They feel themselves to be misunderstood. They confess to being confused about their role and identity. Adolescent Christians, in particular, may feel the additional pressure of being part of a minority group. It would not be surprising if they turned to the picture of Christ who has gone through it all before, as one way of handling such damaging perspectives.

46

A saviour

We asked our interviewees to tell us why they thought Jesus was special for Christians. Their answers focused, though not exclusively, on the death of Christ. A number of these replies took the form of formula statements. Typically these outlined a theory of the atonement and related it to a wider scheme of sin, the fall, judgment and forgiveness. About seven fell into this category. They reflect a particular kind of doctrinal instruction and have the merit, whatever their limitations, of supplying teenagers with a clear-cut, systematic organization of a number of important theological ideas. Unfortunately, like other formulae, they make it difficult for the interviewer to penetrate to the individual's understanding of these ideas.

A much bigger number spoke in general terms about the love of God revealed in the cross without appearing to have any clear theory of atonement in mind. What is significant about their answers, however, is the depth of feeling they communicate. Thirty-four responses indicated a clear understanding that, whatever the theory, the death of Christ had made a relationship with God possible. These ranged from the passionate assertion:

'He was innocent... I don't know why he died.'

through traditional concepts:

'He gave his life as a sacrifice.' 'He died to rid us of sin.' 'He died for our sins.' 'He died on the cross to save us.' 'He died to reconcile us to God.'

to more idiosyncratic interpretations:

'Jesus was like a big dustbin and when he died on the cross it was like all the rubbish in the world had gone into him.'

'He's blasted away the barrier of sin between us and God. I suppose it's more of an invisible force field than anything else... I find this idea of Jesus on the cross with nails through his hands, blood and... I suppose I find it a very vivid image...'

We were taken aback by the intensity of the feeling which they expressed. The picture of Christ on the cross clearly

47

made an impact on a large number of young Christians. But it was the idea of Christ suffering pain on their behalf which seemed to move them. On the whole they did not give an account of why he died. We might say that it is the story of his dying rather than the doctrine of the atonement that captured their imaginations:

'I like going to the stations of the cross. They record different parts of Jesus' passion. And I reach each one and say a special prayer and think of what Jesus went through.'

'He gave up his life. I think I'd ask those who were asking me if they were prepared to give up their life for something.'

'I look up at Jesus on the cross in the stained glass window behind the altar. I try to imagine what he went through.'

'I can really imagine the crucifixion. Sometimes when I'm reading it or accounts of it are being read, sometimes I start crying. I find it very moving and I can see it in my mind.'

'The fact that he underwent that for me and everybody makes me feel sad... Sometimes it makes me feel ashamed that I let him do that.'

'Jesus would have died for me if I'd been the only person on earth.'

'He died for us... I don't think I'd be able to put it as strongly as I feel unless I shout it or something.'

'He never did anything wrong and yet he died for you because he loved you.'

'I've picked the crucifixion because I think it's to do with the nature of man. If a man's in that situation he'd rather lie and save himself than have to go through it. But Christ chose not to.'

The fact that forty-one replies touched on the death of Christ may just be a reflection of its centrality within Christianity, of course. But listening to the statements we were aware of the way in which it was connected to an emphasis on personal forgiveness and acceptance. Here once again the doctrine touched the experience of the adolescent and brought it to life. Jesus wipes the slate clean. Two-thirds of the answers we received stressed the reality of the sense of being forgiven and some of these

48

evidenced a remarkable conviction about eternal life, heaven and hell:

'Click and it's gone like that... If I was knocked down by a bus I'd go straight to heaven.'

'Once you accept him you've got eternal life.'

'I'm not scared of dying. I'll be up with him, y'know.'

'I believe that after I die I will go somewhere where God is.'

'I know I'm going somewhere.'

'I know I'm going to heaven.'

'I don't care two hoots about death.'

These are the cries of the forgiven. These young people spoke as if they had absolute confidence in the forgiving grace of God. They also constituted the majority within the sample. The comments were all the more significant both because they span the denominations and because no question actually required them to speak about forgiveness. In fact many of them proffered their remarks in reply to the question about Christian truths which 'came alive' for them. As far as they were concerned Christian faith was about a Christ who saves and gives assurance of forgiveness. The anxiety shown by Ed was just not typical:

'When I was about nine or ten, I was watching TV and there was this seventy-year-old man on but he had a Teddy Bear—I still have mine I had when I was born; he's all worn now but I still love him—and that man had one. And the thought just hit me, "What's going to happen when I get to his age, when I die?" And that frightens me now, death. That's why I say I'm not a full Christian. Christians should be ready for dying, be ready for it. I don't think I'd stand a fantastic chance of getting into heaven.'

A helper

The final theme which we identified is that of Christ who gives power for daily living. Through him young people can cope with the demands of life. The responses which fell within this category evidenced an ebullient optimism.

49

Twenty-eight of the sixty-seven in the sample specifically mentioned the power of Christ in their lives. It may be slightly artificial to separate this from the resurrection but we wanted to distinguish comments which seemed essentially about the stone, the tomb and the first Easter from those which had a clear contemporary reference:

'He's given us power to be conquerors.'

'Anything good can be done through him and without him it can't be done.'

'Jesus fed five thousand people with just five loaves and two fishes. Well, if I've got that much faith I can do anything.'

'There's this great big muscle man standing there beside you saying, "Well, look, if anything happens, all you've got to do is hold my hand and I'd fight with you."'

Christine had good cause to fasten on Christ as the power of God. In trouble with the police, uncontrollable at home, with a history of glue-sniffing, a suspected pregnancy and five suicide attempts, she spoke quietly but with utter conviction:

'He stopped me. He's just really special in my life. I'll be lost without him.'

Others specified the hope and direction which Christ gives. Life is not meaningless; it is going somewhere and the key to its enigma is to be found in a relationship with Christ:

'I'd say he'd given us a hope to live for. He has given us a reason for living. Non-Christians can't understand why they are in this world. They're here and let's live it to the full and that's it. But we are here to live our lives for God...by the pattern Jesus showed us.'

'He gives us a reason to live. A reason to carry on... It's like a light at the end of the tunnel.'

For the sake of completeness, we need to add the references to Christ's resurrection. Fifteen mentioned the resurrection either as a truth which was significant for them or as one of the reasons why they would say Jesus was special. Once again a case can be made for saying that young Christians are orthodox in their acceptance of the great affirmations of the creed but that the faith comes alive for them when it touches the lives they lead. They agree that 'Christ has risen'; they begin to sparkle when they affirm 'Jesus is alive in me.'

These five themes represent the main emphases in young Christians' understanding of Jesus. A few replies dealt variously with Jesus as one who brings peace and happiness or as revealing a way of life for us to follow—a moral exemplar and guide. Four spoke about the fact that the movement he started was a turning point in history. But most of the responses have been included within the categories already discussed. In conclusion it may be instructive to ask what has been omitted.

Some omissions

Other things could have been said about Jesus which were not mentioned by the young people to whom we spoke. Many referred to the appearance of Jesus and seemed to be basing what they said on the accounts of Jesus' life in the New Testament. But the whole debate about how you handle the Gospels seems to have passed them by. No one appeared to grasp the idea that you have to reconstruct a portrait of Jesus by responsibly studying the texts or even that different Gospels give us different portraits. Their view of Jesus did not seem to be based on any kind of close study of these important accounts. It was couched typically in terms of their private experience—in language which reflects Zeffirelli or insists on the fact that he was 'an ordinary bloke'.

Second, the furore over the public comments of the Bishop of Durham questioning the right way to interpret the accounts of the virgin birth and the resurrection, and the Gospels in general, seemed to have passed them by. We were interviewing at the height of the controversy. The bishop's views and the comments they provoked seemed to be very relevant to the type of questions we were asking. We found only four passing references to the Bishop's views.

Their faith seemed to be quite detached from such current events.

Third, the radical, political Christ failed to make an appearance. The kingdom of God was not mentioned by a single adolescent. We could find no evidence that the teenagers had found in Jesus' teaching the motivation to work for political and social reform.

Fourth, along with this omission must be set the failure to take sufficient account of the demands of discipleship and the suffering inherent in following Jesus. Discipleship was something that Jesus described as taking up the cross— accepting the possibility of being put to death for one's faith. We began to ask if a view of Jesus which effectively ignored this element in his message was really adequate. Their silence on the matter contrasts with the picture they provided, discussed in another chapter, of a demanding God. Perhaps they saw Jesus as a warmer, more approachable figure. It may be that the adolescent need for a friend filtered out the starker parts of the gospel portrait. It may be that they were merely reflecting what they heard in their churches.

5
The Point of Commitment

God wants you to know that he loves you and he wants you to love yourself.

I've just got this sort of inner strength to stop going the bad way.

Today is unquestionably the age of the chat show. Every week on all radio stations and TV channels, someone is interviewing someone else about their life, work and ideas. Many of us are fascinated when the persons being questioned recount some incident or experience which they found particularly memorable for some reason. Telling such stories is something we all love to do. The programme planners are simply cashing in on a very prevalent human pastime. In any pub or club, bus or train, shop or restaurant, at church or at home, wherever people meet, sooner rather than later someone says, 'I must tell you what happened when...'

Everyone has some event or experience in their life which really does matter to them. We wanted to know if the young people in our survey would describe any such happening as of real importance to them, both in leading up to their Christian commitment and consequent upon it. So two of the questions we asked related directly to this issue:

Can you recall any incident or incidents which seem now to be significant in your coming to faith?

What would you pick out as the most significant events or experiences, if any, which have happened to you since you thought of yourself as a Christian?

We were not looking for unusual or startling stories. We were told some remarkable incidents, and a great many more ordinary and straightforward ones. However, we think that every answer to these questions is important. All of the incidents mattered to the tellers. All of them made some contribution to each individual's Christian development. And all of them helped us in our understanding of their Christian life and experience.

Having to answer our questions was also challenging for the teenagers themselves. They found it difficult to explain why they saw the incidents and experiences they described as significant, not least because they had never before been asked for such reasons. Some experiences were memorable but not always easy to analyse or put into words. But the fact that they had been affected enough to recall them in answer to our questions says something about their lives and their Christian values.

We also looked to see if they discerned any pattern to their Christian lives. Were they able to stand back and see in themselves any development or growth to which these incidents had contributed? We did not specifically ask this. Even so, a number of them raised the point, and we shall refer in this chapter to what they said.

We begin by analysing all the different incidents and experiences offered in response to both the questions asked. We shall try to convey the sort of thoughtful and emotional response which the young people indicated that they made to these events. Finally we shall comment on how far they were able to reflect on their experiences, detecting possible patterns of development, signs of growth in their spiritual lives, or perhaps some sensitive understanding of what was happening to them.

Coming to faith

Between them, the sixty-seven young people we interviewed recounted over one hundred incidents that helped them come to accept the Christian faith.

The two most frequently mentioned events were going to a

54

Christian camp or houseparty, and attending a Christian youth group. Thirteen spoke of the first, and twelve mentioned the second. For all of them, the experience challenged either their current beliefs or their lifestyle. In some cases a speaker at one of these events had said something that brought them a fresh insight with a particular message. Sharing thoughts and feelings with Christians of their own age certainly affected many. On other occasions the worship was fresh and special for them. Mandy, a seventeen-year-old minister's daughter, made this comment:

'We used to get up and dance and sing and really pray. And I wish sometimes that our church was like that. It was great and I loved it. You know, just singing and dancing and praising. It was fantastic.'

Paul, who is now a member of a Leeds Pentecostal church, had found his church youth group to be highly influential in bringing him to faith:

'Yes, it sounds daft but the way I became a Christian was through Crusaders, and the way I was dragged along to Crusaders initially was through my elder brother. I'd been going to church all my life and I was totally against church because I found it all so boring, and when I was old enough to decide for myself, I decided that this wasn't for me.'

But he went, and the positive impression made on him by some of his brother's friends there kept him going there until he grew into faith.

In nine cases the really critical incident was a special Christian rally, such as those conducted by the travelling evangelists Billy Graham and Luis Palau for example. The music, the atmosphere, the large crowds, the powerful preaching all helped to make them memorable. Others instanced Christian music concerts, a special service or sermon in church, a first Holy Communion service, just going to a church for the first time, or leaving one church to attend another 'which was more alive'.

The key event for one girl was the sudden conversion of her mother. This event affected her deeply, and it was not long before she made her own commitment to Christ. For seventeen-year-old Penny, watching the film *Jesus of Nazareth* had a profound effect:

'For years people had told me, "Jesus has died for you so you can be forgiven now." But I'd never really understood the magnificence of his death, if you see what I mean—the strength of it. And I saw it on this film and it just hit me like a brick—you know, actually seeing him die. It was awful. And I wept for hours that night.'

Heather's critical incident came at her confirmation in her local Roman Catholic church:

'I think then I realized what I was taking on, that I was taking more on. I had made a decision to stick to religion. I was sixteen.'

The fact that some of her friends were telling her 'it's not worth it' probably made the event even more important for her. Another Liverpool seventeen-year-old, Julie, had a very different experience to recount:

'Well, when I was born, the doctors didn't think I would live the night, but I was baptized that night, and that has always been a sort of sign to me.'

Further answers referred to specific help from parents, or discussions with friends who were already Christians. Two said that reading something from the Bible had been of particular help, while three others told us that they had had certain prayers answered. As one said:

'I really prayed about that job, and when he answered, that really helped my faith.'

Lastly, two more spoke very warmly about the influence of Christian teachers. Anne described the incident that stood out for her as follows:

'I think it was the way Mrs X talked about Jesus being in her life and God being alive that impressed me. I knew that in my mind, but I didn't really understand it. I did know that I wanted Jesus to be alive in my life, and I wanted the things that were happening to her to happen to me. One thing I remember, she drew two circles on the board. One was the world and the other

one represented heaven, and where they overlapped, she said that's where the Christians were and where she was. And that was where I wanted to be too.'

The main point about all these answers is that these experiences all showed Christianity to the young people not as something dull or as an escape from reality, but as life-enhancing and very attractive.

Other incidents

A variety of other answers was given to us. For seventeen-year-old Alan, having to change school at thirteen proved memorable. He went to church 'because I liked the music and I sang in the choir'. But at his new school, it was 'meeting other Christians and realizing that being a Christian actually meant living it out and not just going to church and going through the motions' that eventually led to his making a real commitment.

Melanie had vastly more traumatic experiences. She had been forced to leave home because of drinking and glue-sniffing, and on a trip back from the addiction unit someone on the minibus took the wheel from the driver and crashed the bus, killing one of Melanie's friends and injuring Melanie. She had been to hospital before this, when she had tried to commit suicide, and it was there that she met a Christian nurse who was to play a crucial part in her life, writing regularly to her, then inviting her to her home, leading her to Christ, and befriending her ever after.

Five young people referred to family problems—in one case, the parents divorcing, in three others, illness and death—as significant. Another said that changing to the 'O' level course on religious education played a key part in his Christian experience. Yet another confessed that it was being made to face up to the prospect of leaving school, and the real fear of life after school that this engendered, which led to seeking help from religion. And for one sixteen-year-old girl, one memorable incident was hearing an eight-year-old child give a testimony on the Sunday television programme 'Songs of Praise'.

Only four of the young people interviewed could not offer any early incident which they regarded as important, a finding we think is quite remarkable.

Growing in faith

Fifteen of the teenagers had no answer to give us to this question. Their inability to recount any later event of significance to them was not surprising when it is remembered that around a quarter of all those contacted had regarded themselves as Christians for less than a year at the time they were interviewed. However, all the others had at least one incident to share. Altogether eighty-two examples were given to us.

The two sorts of event most frequently mentioned were, first, large Christian conventions of the kind which usually take place at holiday times and attract people from all over the country—the Dales Bible Week, Splashdown, and most of all Spring Harvest were referred to—and, second, parish weekends and church houseparties. One factor which made these occasions remarkable for Nick, sixteen, and Mike, fifteen, was the presence of very large numbers of other young Christians. About Spring Harvest Liz said:

'It was important because it did give me a tremendous push, and it opened my eyes to some things that I hadn't noticed before, and also to things I had, but wasn't too sure about. And also things that I knew very well but were sort of reaffirmed and looked at from a different angle.'

She gave examples from the worship and the seminars and finally commented:

'I think it made me grow deeper into God's word and also closer to him in certain aspects that I wasn't previously.'

These comments sum up those of most who referred to this kind of event.

For Hilary and Keith, going to Lourdes had a similarly

deep effect. Hilary emphasized that it strengthened her faith a lot:

'I really enjoyed it, you know. It made everything so much more important. When I came back, I enjoyed church much more. And I took a lot more notice. It's an experience and you get closer to everyone. You come back and I think it makes you grow up a lot.'

Keith would agree with that:

'Going down on the bus we have mass every day and prayers in the evening, so it was very intensive, I mean Roman Catholic religious intensive, but you get used to it after a bit, and it doesn't become a drag because it's so different from normal procedures anyway. It seems very much more from the inside, not from a book.'

Eighteen-year-old Derek, who was particularly enthusiastic about his church's parish weekends and about Dales Week, put it this way:

'You felt you could release yourself more. And you could really learn about God more, and learn a few lessons.'

One lesson he said he had learned was that he was 'baptized in the Holy Spirit and speaking in tongues'. Baptism in the Holy Spirit was frequently mentioned, ten referring to it. This experience has been described as an encounter with God in which Christians receive the supernatural power of the Holy Spirit into their lives to equip them for service to God. Before she cited this experience, seventeen-year-old Kathy told us how for three years after making her commitment public she really struggled, and did not try to witness at all:

'Nothing, nothing really happened for years, for three years, until I realized that there was something called 'baptism in the Spirit'. When I got baptized—I moved church and I got baptized at a Pentecost meeting—and, my goodness, then I was raring to go.'

Large Christian rallies and missions in the local church proved to be helpful in deepening the faith of some of the young people. For seven interviewees their being baptized

59

was an important step in their spiritual growth, and in five cases the baptism was by total immersion. Several of the people in this group also had to say something about their faith to the rest of the church at the time of their baptism, so the event was doubly significant. Three others stated that moving to a different church after becoming more committed was a very important stage in their development, while two others were much affected listening to the testimony of new Christians in their churches. Both said it reawakened them to renewed dedication.

Many raised the subject of prayer in their answers. Ten referred to prayer meetings they had attended, and found them significant occasions. Mike said:

'*We share everything, thoughts, problems, desires and things. Then we sort of share all our feelings. Then we pray, and God really seems to answer our prayers. I can't somehow explain, but he does.*'

Many others stressed to us how important to their spiritual growth answered prayer had been. One or two, such as Graham, said they had asked for specific signs and received them. Paul, when sixteen, was given a difficult task by his boss after an argument at work:

'*I thought I could do a certain job this way, which was the best way, and the new boss thought it was best doing it a different way, a way I didn't like. He tried to prove me wrong and I just stopped in the warehouse and prayed: "Please help me this time,"—and I'm talking about five or six hundred pieces of paper. The one I needed was only two or three sheets further on, that's all. I just shouted: "Praise the Lord."*'

Steve's example is especially dramatic. His straight-forward account heightens the drama:

'*It was one night up at the youth club, you know, a disco and that. And I remember reading the Bible where the fellow tells you that whatever you ask in the Lord's name, he promises you'll receive, right? ... And as we were coming out there was about eleven lads waiting for us, you know. And they all had big sticks and clubs and that. They were just down the road, and I*

60

just says, "Well, Lord, you promised this... I'm not going to run. You keep us safe like. I'm going to trust you, you know. I'm definitely not going to run." As I was walking, I was saying, "Well, put it this way. If you don't keep us safe, then you're not real. 'Cos you've gone back on your word." 'Cos I'd asked in his name, you know.

'So I was just standing... and I never got hurt, you know. They started to come over. They all had big sticks and they were all much bigger than us. So as they came over the road, everyone that was with me scattered... and I wasn't expecting them to run, I tell you the truth. I was just left on my own, you know. I used to be a skinhead. You wouldn't think I was a tearaway, like. And I just thought to myself, "Well, Lord, you promised." And there was a kid came at us. He went at us, like. I was pressed against the fence, you know. And he just stopped for no reason. He just said, "Aw, go on, get yourself away." He said something like "You're too young." After that night I just knew... He couldn't hit us. I just know it, you know. He just couldn't hit us. And after that I really grew, grew from that.'

Many different personal experiences were mentioned, such as becoming a server, making a first confession, speaking in tongues, speaking at youth meetings, helping at Christian holiday camps for inner city children, reading Christian books and persuading a friend to go to church. Barry's story was definitely personal and unusual. He'd gone to a camp with friends and one evening they began to pray for people they knew. He continued:

'You know when people say they've got the fear of God in them? Well, that's what I got. I was absolutely terrified. I was just sitting there and had my eyes closed and this voice in my head said, "Open your eyes." I opened my eyes, and this was the truth—if you want to doubt us you can—there was an angel sitting beside us and two more sitting in front of us, and I thought "Oh no, what's these? Are they ghosts or what?" Then I realized what they were and I went "Cor, lad!" I just sat there and went "Ohhh." Then I said, "Oh, that's brilliant, that," and then I closed my eyes, and opened them again and they were

gone. And that really showed us that he is alive. I was full of joy at what I had seen, and I was dead surprised that he showed three angels to me... I couldn't really describe it.'

Other incidents

One important event for one sixteen-year-old girl, mentioned in the first chapter, was bringing to an end a formerly close contact with a woman who indulged in intensive occult practices. Breaking off this relationship also resulted in freedom from the fear that the occult had created in her. Another interesting example was given to us by Barbara, who was greatly challenged not long after becoming a Christian by the loss of her two closest friends who both left the area:

'I found that really hard,' 'cos I depended on them an awful lot for support and friendship. So when they left, I really had to realize where I stood and whether it was faith—whether I was relying on God or them. That was a big step, 'cos I really had to grow as a person, and become strong.'

A very different incident was recounted by Penny. She was praying with the woman who led her Christian youth group when this lady suddenly said:

"'I've got a picture from God and it's of you, and you're starving and naked, and I've just realized you've been starved of love all these years." And it was true. I broke down and cried, because she'd just hit it on the head, really because I was just the loneliest person in the world. And she said, "God wants you to know that he loves you and he wants you to love yourself." And so I stopped being lonely from then.'

Another moving incident was shared by Gina, aged seventeen. This was the death of the mother of one of her best friends:

'She was so young and had a daughter and two sons. The fact that God could do that, I mean take somebody away when he could have picked someone else. But people like me, I suppose, could understand that that's the way it was, and that everything

was for a good reason, although at the time it didn't seem so, and it probably wouldn't go against the family, and that made you realize and accept it. I was fifteen at the time when that happened.'

On a more cheerful note, eighteen-year-old Wendy told us she'd had a lot of experiences of joy:

'I remember just very little things like when my friend came in once and we'd had a prayer meeting at my house and it just felt like the room was filled with the presence—and it was really God, and it was beautiful. And then I think there were times when my friends have rung—we've been praying for friends to become Christians—and they've rung and shown signs [of deepening interest].'

Elaine from Liverpool should have the final comment on all these incidents. Her thinking was coloured by the fact that her sister had been divorced when Elaine herself was just twelve. Five years later she spoke like this:

'I think for most people it's significant events in your life that lead you up to wanting to be nearer and nearer to him all the time, because he's really the only person you find comforting. So I think it's when things happen in your own family or within your own environment, that's when you really feel, and that's when you really come close to God.'

Elaine's comment is unusual in that not many of the young people reflected like that upon the incidents they described to us. But a number did say why the events mattered to them. We have quoted one or two examples. The response of others is also enlightening.

Graham spoke like this about listening to a talk on the crucifixion:

'Something just hit you. And I felt from then on something had changed and I knew it had changed.'

Debby, at a rally in Newcastle led by former teenage gangster-turned-evangelist Nicky Cruz said of the call to go forward and commit her life to Jesus:

'It just struck me to the heart and I could do nothing but go up there.'

Stewart commented about a church service, 'I felt he was just talking directly to me.' Changing church was important to Derek because 'before going to X I didn't know you needed to get saved'. Going to church at all was significant for fifteen-year-old Tricia because she was surprised how friendly the Christians there were, accepting her readily. And when Christine heard Billy Graham preach at Roker Park, she 'knew it was the beginning of something new, and I wanted to carry on'.

Pat's more unusual pre-commitment experience was being slain in the Spirit at a special healing service in her Roman Catholic church in Middlesbrough. This is an experience in which the person falls to the ground under the power of the Holy Spirit, and is a phenomenon found in every period of Christian church history and across all the denominations. It is particularly associated with times of renewal and revival. Pat stated:

'I really felt rested, just completely rested. It was definitely a filled sort of experience. And nothing really mattered (not even the fact that she was confused and could not move). All that mattered was just a state of complete restful ecstasy. You just rest on this pure God sort of thing.'

Two frequent reasons offered to explain why incidents were seen as critical were that through the experiences they learned more about God and Christianity and that, as Tricia put it, 'I felt God to be a lot closer'. Mike declared: 'I've just got this sort of inner strength to stop going the bad way. I do feel I'm a lot closer to God and feel more assured.' Emma valued the talks she heard at a weekend houseparty because 'they made me sit up and think', while a sermon was important for Laura because 'I had a fantastic feeling when he was preaching'. A particular mission at her church mattered to Debby 'because things weighing on me and my Christian life were sorted out and dealt with, like the question of sin and everything'. And a particular church service was significant for Ian because the realization came forcefully to him that 'he's given us the power to be more than conquerors.

You've got this power in you through Jesus.'

Fifteen-year-old Alison was baptized when she was eight. This was a key event for her 'because I knew I was obeying what Christ wanted me to do'. She stressed that she did it for him, not because people wanted her to. Ruth was given the chance to help at a houseparty. 'That was a real event for me,' she said. 'I could see myself growing in confidence.' Michelle found a Christian holiday remarkable because 'when I stay with people, I find I'm loving them a lot more'. Richard told us he was uplifted by seeing people changed at a church meeting, and thus encouraged 'to continue trusting God's good will'. As Gina explained in a comment with which most of our sample would heartily agree, 'Incidents like that change you, give you a different view, a different outlook on life.'

Signs of growth

There remains the question of whether these young people showed any ability to see in all these incidents any pattern of growth or development in their spiritual lives. Most of them were very new to the Christian faith. As mentioned earlier, some had acknowledged themselves to be Christians for less than a year when we met them. It is not surprising, therefore, that many had no answer to our question about incidents since they came to faith. Nor is it surprising that only a small number appeared to be reflecting on their experiences in any depth. We felt that many were taking their lives for granted, reacting to events as they came along, but not really anticipating, or showing much sensitive understanding. Rather, most of them were simply enjoying their faith and trusting God to take care of their future.

But a few of them were thinking more deeply about their lives. David, aged seventeen, began his answer to our question like this:

'The first significant incidents were little steps really. You keep going up one stage further, tiny little things that you don't

often even realize, although often it's a conscious effort to get rid of something in your life to encourage something else that you know you should be doing. And you can feel something coming back from the work you're putting in to it. Of the steps throughout my life, the first little one was reading the Book of Revelation, and this was all on my own, without any outside help as it were, and there was that day where I was determined to start really working instead of just slagging along having just a little head knowledge. That was it, and then I started feeling the Spirit working within me but it wasn't any very great power or anything.'

But each 'little step' helped him to grow in understanding. Anne had a longer perspective:

'Whenever I have a spiritual birthday—I'm three now—I sort of look back, and see how far I've come and what's happened in the last year. The way Jesus is taking more of me. You can see different patterns of thought. Different things you know. The way you've changed over the last three years. It's probably a lot to do with growing up anyway, but being more mature and having different outlooks on my future, what I'm going to do with my life and how I'm going to use it for God's glory.'

Having prayer answered was one crucial event for Mary. A friend of hers made a commitment to Christ and at the end it was very emotional:

'But at the same time I knew it wasn't just emotional. I knew that the Spirit was moving. And I felt like I was growing. And I learned so much from the Bible studies. One night I said, "Well Lord, I'm going to this school and I want you to use me to witness. I want you to get me to the right people to talk to at the right time." And I suddenly began to realize my Christian purpose.'

Finally, Kathy described going to Spain for a month as 'the most testing time of my life'. But this led 'to the highest point in my Christian life, of baptism. But I believe the Lord took me through that wilderness to really assure me that he did exist, so that the baptism would be all the more, if you understand.'

6

Someone to Turn To

When you needed help he was always there, and if he said he'd do something for you, he always would, and he'd never let you down.

...unless they actually show you God's love, you can't really accept it.

Becoming a Christian is a bit like getting married—you suddenly acquire a completely new set of relatives and friends. All at once, a whole lot of people begin to react towards you in a different way. You are accepted and welcomed in new places, and made to feel even more at home in settings already familiar to you. Lots more people seem to take a fresh interest in you and in your new status. They want to know how you are getting on and how they can help. Even people who have grown up in the church but who make a new, personal commitment can find that the quality of their relationships with other members of the church deepens dramatically.

Most of the young people we contacted were intrigued and pleased by this kind of Christian experience. Usually without prompting, they spoke of people who had influenced them and who were important to them. Even so, we felt this was a subject to be opened up by a specific question. We wanted to know who these significant people were and what influence they had. What sort of role did they play and why were they seen as significant?

We wondered what qualities our young people looked for and found in them, and whether, for some at least, their own profession of faith was really due to some friend with great charisma and influence rather than genuine personal commitment. As this chapter indicates, Christianity is demonstrated to teenagers by a wide range of people, usually friendly, sincere, and, for the most part, very ordinary. The chapter also shows, as do most of the other quotations in the book, that the faith of the young people we questioned is real and genuine.

Obviously, for some young people, their parents and others in the family circle are the crucial influences. But many of them came from non-Christian backgrounds. So where did they come into contact with these Christians who were to be so important to them? Why was the initial contact made and how did it develop?

All parents of teenagers wonder about the people their offspring meet outside the home. The trouble is that when they ask questions, this interest is sometimes interpreted as an interrogation, and the answers become non-committal, censored, or even non-existent. But that kind of reaction is not inevitable. To any parents of Christian teenagers who happen to read this book, we predict that if they asked their young people the questions we asked ours, concerning 'significant others', if their teenagers were willing to share with them, most responses would be similar to ours. Their experience of 'significant' Christians would be like those of the teenagers in our sample. We want to highlight three questions about such people.

Who are they?

Obviously the first question we must ask is: Who are these people whose influence was felt to be important before, and after, the acknowledgment of Christian commitment? Eight sorts of people were described, and many teenagers mentioned more than one, a few noting as many as three or four.

The most common answer was 'parents', over half our sample making reference to either their mother or father, or both. The next most frequent reply (from twenty-eight teenagers) referred to their Christian friends, by whom they meant friends at school, fellow students, or social friends, people of around their own age. Seventeen replies concerned youth leaders, of whom most would be in their twenties at the time. Thirteen mentioned a member of the clergy, and eleven indicated relatives other than their parents. Adult Christians, such as family friends or church elders, were also listed by eleven young people, and eight others spoke of teachers at school who were a Christian influence. The eighth and last answer we received—from seven young people—referred to 'the whole church family', and we feel it is proper to include this answer with the others.

How did the young people come into contact with these 'significant people'? As far as parents and other relatives are concerned, the answer is obvious. And in some cases it was through family connections and activities like church-going that some met youth leaders or a minister or other adult Christians. But many teenagers were befriended by contacts at school or work, and introduced to other Christians through them. Occasionally one of the young people in our sample had made the first approach towards, or had simply met at special events or during some incident in their lives, individuals who were to become important to them.

But once contact was made, what happened next? After all, not every child from a Christian home becomes a committed Christian. And a great many young people in the course of daily life become acquainted with Christians, and yet are not affected as were those in our sample. Hence our second key question, which refers to the role these 'significant others' played, and usually still were playing, in the lives of these young people.

What role do they play?

In almost every example we were given, consistency was a key quality. Also, contact was (and is) continuous. A few did refer to individuals whose impact was made only before conversion—such as visiting speakers—and one or two others spoke of people who assumed importance in their lives once their commitment was made known. But most individuals described to us were, and continued to be, always available.

Five main roles can be identified, and many of these important people mattered to these young Christians because they fulfilled more than one such part.

Perhaps the most influential one for many was that of setting an example. Tom, from Liverpool, said this of his parents:

'Without actually forcing me to become a Christian, they have shown me what it is to be a Christian. Like my dad going to mass every Sunday. Without telling me, he's shown me how to be a Christian in a certain sense, and that means a lot because, without forcing me, he's shown me in his own way how a Christian should act.'

Anne from Wales described one of her teachers at school:

'I was really impressed by her because she really showed that there was something, and I liked what she had and I wanted it.'

Mike from Durham described his youth leader as important:

'He was a really good Christian—not good in inverted commas, but a good Christian. And he was really Spirit-filled in the meetings.'

It was because of the example set by this man that Mike began to go to see him privately for help.

Sixteen-year-old Rebecca from Sunderland commended her parents as 'a great example', but not the most important:

'It was the young people more than anything. They just appeared to be such people as I wanted to get to know better. They were a really good example, because they showed that you can really have fun even if you are a Christian. You're not boring, even if you are classed as boring.'

Mike's youth leader was one of those who played the

second key role most effectively, the role of listener and confidant. So was Emma's mother, about whom her daughter said, 'I've always confided in her about everything. She's open with me and I'm open with her.' In Hilary's case it was 'my Nan. She's always someone I can talk to when everyone else sort of wants to back out, or laugh at me, or something.' Fifteen-year-old Tricia had no such source in her home background, but she found help with a family at church, especially the husband. This man, a farmer in his mid-forties, was the one who befriended her:

'He started asking me to come to the church. When I first went, I was a bit upset because my parents wouldn't go, and aren't saved, and I used to feel that all the world was on my shoulders, so I'd just talk to Bill about it and he really helped me. And he's even been round to see my mum. You can always turn to him, and his wife's nice as well.'

Mark, also fifteen, was a member of a small prayer group, and he relied heavily on his friends there to listen and help:

'When we first started off (after encouragement to do so by their youth leader) we were all really apprehensive about sharing anything, but it's far more open now. We share any problems, encouragements, or any thoughts we've generally had over the last few days. We discuss them and pray about them.'

We happen to know another member of this group, a year older than Mark, and he confirmed how they get on 'really honestly with each other, and very deeply'.

Young Christians need affirmation and encouragement. Fortunately these young people had met people who fulfilled this need. The role of encourager is a crucial one, and this was especially vital for Melanie who, before becoming a Christian, had experienced much trauma and rejection. Her 'significant person' was a lady about ten years older than herself. She told us a great deal about this person, who, she said, 'was always ready to sit and listen'. But more important still:

'She makes you feel as if you're wanted. She's given me more love than anyone in my life.'

71

Alan from Leeds made a similar point. Some of the important people in his life were the sixth formers who ran the school Christian group, and who 'gave you a real sense that they were interested in you, and of them trying to help.'

David remarked, 'You can't get all the help you need from just one person. You do need a group of friends.' He then spoke of two girls 'who gave me a lot of encouragement whenever I was speaking to them'. He explained that 'when we're on almost exactly the same level in Christianity, we could speak really freely about things and learn from each other in everything we did'. Ed, on the other hand, received most encouragement from the curate at his church. 'I can talk to him about anything at all. His house is open any time.' As a young Christian, Ed admitted he had lots of problems about belief and practice, and this curate constantly helped him along.

This last point leads naturally on to the fourth key role of these 'significant people', that of teacher or information giver. Very few people become Christians without having been told something about Christianity and, once committed, further instruction and guidance are essential for growth and development. Many of the young people interviewed commented on this, and acknowledged their debt to the people they told us about.

For example, Peter's remark about his youth group leaders, that 'they could explain about Christianity and make it lively and interesting', was echoed a number of times by others. Barbara said of her school friends that 'they helped me and explained things I didn't understand before'. Many spoke of their debt to their parents in this regard. Debby described how her parents taught her gently and prayed regularly with her from her earliest years, and other parents helped their children to comprehend biblical and church teaching. Jill gave her mother much credit for helping her to understand about Christian matters both before and after her own commitment:

'*It's just always been a suggestion which I've picked up each step of the way. So as she's given me more information I've, like a sponge, absorbed it all and hopefully taken it in, and put it into practice.*'

Sometimes the parental approaches varied. One parent would be helpful and informative; the other less so or not at all. Or, as Gina told us, there might be a difference between the two parents:

'*My mum forced the issue, but my dad didn't. My mum, she says, I want you to go and be instructed. But I think really that perhaps it was my dad who helped me most because he didn't force anything on me. He invited you to think about what was right but he didn't put any pressure on you.*'

Tim said much the same thing about his youth leader, and added this comment:

'*Looking back, what he in fact did was to sort of drag us along in his spiritual slipstream. And we got a fair grounding in what it was all about.*'

We liked the remark sixteen-year-old Kirsty made about her rector:

'*He puts less into my head in sermons but makes me think out for myself what he was saying or how I should act or react towards people.*'

We also think it is worth quoting Elaine in full:

'*I think your mum and dad obviously have got a lot to do with it, because they take you from a very young age and breed it into you very early. And I think the teachers especially are very important as well. At your junior age you can be influenced a lot by your teachers and what they think and, you know, "Whatever Miss says must be true," sort of thing. But as you get older, it's different kinds of relationships, and perhaps it's more important because you study each other's point of view then. And even if you disagree with what your friends think, it's important that you understand what they think and that you can see their attitude, even though you might not agree. And it's important that they also see your point of view. And I suppose it's also very important—it's a kind of mark of maturity—that*' *you don't rebuff anybody for their feelings and attitudes, but you take the time to listen to one another because it's the only way you're going to learn anything at all. But it's the people you're in contact with all the time that you're going to learn off—your parents, your teachers, and your friends.'*

After being an example, a good listener, encourager and teacher, one last role was that of supporter. This involved standing alongside, sharing experiences, defending, and just being there. Many of the teenagers still at school were grateful for the support of their Christian friends there. As Mary told us:

'We've talked about things, and it's the way we've grown together. It's been wonderful. I was the sort of person who felt very alone in life before, and I thought I couldn't tell my friends, and I had to take all my problems on myself. Now I know Jesus is helping us and I'm not on my own any more.'

All the young people who referred to the whole church family as significant said or implied the same thing. And John said this of his youth group leader:

'When you needed help he was always there, and if he said he'd do something for you, he always would, and he'd never let you down.'

At times, this support was quite costly for those giving it. It might involve criticism from those at home, school or society who were hostile to Christianity. It also always meant giving up personal free time—to spend time with young people, to go on holiday with them, to keep in regular touch over a long period of time, and to open their homes to them.

What are they like?

So we come to the third key question about these 'significant people'. What sort of people were they? What qualities stood out? What made them special? The same characteristics were referred to again and again in discussing the eight groups of people that were described to us.

Perhaps the most important one was being loving and

caring. Emma's testimony about her mother was that 'she's warm, friendly, and she loves everybody'. Mike spoke similarly about his youth leader: 'He's got a real deep love for everyone.' Becky's comment about her youth leaders was equally emphatic: 'They just keep loving everybody, no matter what they do or have done.'

This kind of comment was also made by all those who spoke of their church family as being important to them. Richard experienced this both before and after he made his commitment. Indeed, it contributed strongly to the decision he duly made. He said: 'I just felt loved and accepted like I'd never felt before.' Some of the young people could be quite critical of church and church members, but they were also grateful, and would, in the main, agree with one sixteen-year-old's statement that 'there is so much love there...there really is'.

Melanie's summary of the older Christian who had done so much for her, that 'she's warm, understanding and sympathetic', referred to traits also commonly mentioned. Generous, helpful, kind, considerate, patient, friendly and understanding were other descriptions we heard again and again. Most of these 'significant others' also had the ability to make the teenagers feel that they mattered.

'*He really got alongside of us and befriended us, and he had a really big influence on us, and just made us feel accepted.*'

'*He never forced me and he never turned me away.*'

'*He was very understanding and patient. I felt he was really interested in me as a person.*'

Alison told us that her parents were always available if she had a problem:

'*I could go to them always and talk to them about it, and I know they won't tell me what to do, but just advise me.*'

Beth described an adult Christian who was similarly always there when needed:

'*Mrs. T. was so willing, so generous, so kind to help. She'd do anything for you. Whenever you met her you'd feel her warmth generate through to you.*'

75

As Andy said of his teacher, 'she never rejected anyone'. And from what he told us, this lady had a great deal to put up with from him.

Other qualities were consistency and trustworthiness. The young people all knew that their 'significant others' could be relied upon to receive them willingly, to keep the confidences they shared, and to be loyal and faithful. They were never unpredictable or insincere. As Sally said of her Christian school teachers, 'It's the way they are so steadfast, never wavering, and always the same.'

One further characteristic, a kind of special personal serenity, is worthy of mention, even though the young people who cited it found it hard to describe. Listen to Louise talking about her Christian neighbours:

'I remember there was this preacher once who said you can tell when somebody's got Jesus inside them because you can see him looking out at people. Well, there was just something about them. Even though I was so young and I'd never experienced very much in the world, I knew they had something.'

Andy told us of a nun who taught him:

'She had something going. She had something that was special. That got to me and I respected it. She was probably the shining personality who influenced me. And she never ever went sort of spare, or berserk. She never ever got on her high horse. And it's not only me. She was like it with anybody.'

Another special teacher was Kathy's:

'Mrs. H.'s face...it's... I can't describe it. It's just radiant. I wish I had a face like that. It's shining. Even Mum noticed it. It just shines with God's glory, and even when she's not smiling, she's got authority.'

We would also like to quote part of a long description given to us by Pat, concerning her great aunt, with whom she used to stay from time to time:

'There was such a peaceful atmosphere in that house. And it was like she had this really simple acceptance of her faith, you know, and she didn't question it, and she didn't need to make it complicated. She just accepted what came along, and she was

76

just happy to be plodding off to mass to be involved with all the ladies of the parish to make tea for people and this, that and the other. And that just stayed with me. I never realized until afterwards why I'd never kicked out at going to church, but it was looking back on it that I realized that her simple acceptance made me go along with it. It gave me this kind of feeling inside me that was just gentle and just a sort of beginning seed.'

What all teenagers value greatly is understanding, openness and acceptance of themselves for what and who they are. What they all most need is unconditional love, affirmation, and teaching, though they do not always recognize that last requirement. They also need to know where they stand in any relationship, and therefore consistency in reception and treatment is also essential. If these needs are not met, their growth to maturity will be stunted. It seems as though the young, middle-aged and sometimes elderly people described to us were, by and large, meeting these needs in the teenagers.

The young people were a very mixed group. Some came from very secure and loving homes. Others, from what they said, had a more mixed and less certain upbringing. And of these, some had had very damaging and wounding experiences. For them, most of all, those Christians who had become so important to them were literally their life-savers, or life-renewers. Through their new-found faith, and the constant help and example of these Christian friends and leaders, their lives had more purpose. They were also realizing more clearly their own worth and value.

All the young people would testify to that last point. And that is due in no small measure to their 'significant others'. They recognized these people as genuine, with a genuine interest in them. They showed by their nature and their consistent actions that they regarded young people as important. Not surprisingly, everything the young people said about them emphasizes that it is what they are that made the impact. It provided the opening to the relationships they established and the continuing influence they had. Once

77

again, as Barry said of the man he was describing to us, 'there was just something about him'.

We think it is important to stress one other quality of these Christian parents, relatives, friends, leaders, pastors and teachers, which can be deduced from what was said about so many of them. There was a self-sacrificing aspect to their relationships with the young people. They were clearly willing regularly and consistently to make time for them, to share their homes and activities with them, and to persist with the relationship even when sometimes rebuffed or disappointed or let down.

If the question is asked, 'Why was this so?', we think Penny gave the answer in something she said about her Christian youth leader. Her words also sum up everything we were told about those who mattered to the young people in their Christian lives:

'I think he was the person who showed me, in an active way, God's love. You know, people can talk about it until they're blue in the face, but unless they actually show you God's love, you can't really accept it.'

7

The Company of Believers

I see the small group of friends that I meet to pray with as being the church.

What I look for most is what God, Jesus, is going to teach us. Even though that's sometimes a bit heavy going.

I just remind myself that church isn't a club.

There is a commonly accepted stereotype of the relationship between young people and the Christian church which runs something like this: Adolescents are deeply alienated from the church. They find sermons boring, services monotonous and clergymen disapproving, infantile and out of touch. They are bitterly conscious of the generation gap between themselves and the fuddy-duddies who fill the pews. They need to be wooed with livelier services, louder music, more colloquial language and promises of greater involvement. Acts of worship will only hold the young in so far as they concentrate on 'performance' aspects, approximating more closely to the concert or the disco. The life of the local congregation is not relevant to the teenage Christian. He or she is likely to be attracted either to the large scale 'celebration' or the intimate 'cell' provided by the youth fellowship.

It is not difficult to find reports which give colour to these statements. The influential Martin and Pluck survey commented: 'In general the image that our young people had of the church as a building was not one to attract them— grey, cold, empty, or alternatively full of boring, middle-aged respectable people all listening or pretending to listen to boring sermons from the "vicar".[1] 'There is a very strong feeling that going to church simply isn't a normal, expected part of being a healthy, ordinary adolescent.'[2]

We were interested in how this group of teenagers would match up to such a stereotype. We asked them what they found especially helpful or significant in services of worship whether in church or elsewhere. As part of the answer they told us about the types of services or parts of services that had meant a lot to them. We also asked if there was anything about church worship that they actually disliked or did not find particularly helpful or significant. It was our hope that these questions would allow them freedom to pick out aspects of church life which really mattered to them, whether for praise or blame, without feeling that we were directing their responses. However, we added another question: Are there things that you make a conscious effort to do or to think about when you go to church? The intention here was to catch something of their understanding of what worship was and to see how far they engaged in it in a serious and active way.

Before looking in detail at the results of our inquiries, we ought to note two things. First, the group of people that we selected cannot be seen as representative of the whole adolescent population. As we have said before, the teenagers were selected principally on the grounds that they perceived themselves as committed to the church. Such a group will obviously be more explicitly Christian than the fifteen-to-eighteen age group generally. They are also more likely to have positive attitudes to their churches than those who attend infrequently or only through association with a uniformed youth organization or as a result of parental pressure or who are beginning to drop out. Nevertheless, the young people do represent an important constituency and one that has been under-researched.

Second, Martin and Pluck claimed to have discovered that denominational affiliation was irrelevant in their study of young people's beliefs. We interviewed across the denominations—from Roman Catholic and Anglican to Brethren, Pentecostal and house-church. In one sense denominations did seem to be of slight significance. There was remarkable agreement on their understanding of what worship was, their likes and dislikes, and even on their personal lists of dos and don'ts. However, the culture of each denomination became apparent in the examples they gave and the traditions they observed. Martin and Pluck stated, for example, that only one adolescent spoke warmly of the 'traditions and sacraments of our church' and mentioned that her father had brought her up to love them.[3] We suspect that this conclusion will need to be qualified somewhat. According to our sample, teenage Christians do have a respect for the traditions of their churches.

How do they see the church?

As far as we could discover, young Christians were favourably disposed towards their churches. Out of sixty-seven replies, thirty-seven were unequivocally positive. Indeed some of the comments were almost embarrassingly so:

'Now I can't wait to get there.' 'I like it all really.' 'I love it round church.' 'Ninety per cent of the things are helpful.' 'It was the church that made me grow fast.' 'There is a good atmosphere in St John's.' 'The Spirit almost hits you in the face.'

About fifteen replies could be described as basically negative in attitude. Even here, though, it is worth analysing the reasons which were given. Three were negative about the churches in which they had grown up but were appreciative of the churches to which they had transferred. These replies should probably be categorized as positive. Three compared their church unfavourably with their youth group. Only nine made the sort of criticisms cited in Martin and Pluck.

About ten evidenced a 'mixed' attitude towards the church. To be fair, though, the balance of their remarks was positive. For example, one spoke warmly of the communion service at her church while wanting more times of quiet. Another was critical of her priest's inability to establish personal relationships but expressed commitment to the people as the body of Christ. A third was put off by 'high language' but valued the communion services.

Is there a generation gap?

The idea of a generation gap is made up of a number of elements. It includes the assumption that young people have no time for the older members of the church, and that they in their turn are hostile, apprehensive and critical. It takes for granted the idea that these two groups scarcely talk to each other. Adolescents are expected to make dismissive comments about the services in general and sermons and preachers in particular. They will complain that they lack a voice in decision-making and are seldom asked to participate in the conduct of worship. When they do take responsibility for a service, it will be seen as an opportunity to drag the church into the twentieth century, to wake people up briefly before they sink back into slumber until the next youth event. They will show little sense of commitment to the church or the congregation; their primary loyalty will be to their peer group or the para-church organization.

Some of the young people we interviewed fitted this picture fairly closely:

'*I must admit I don't like church because at the minute I'm finding it pretty boring... I've told Dad what I think about the church and why I don't go, and that I think church is not for youth but for people older than us.*'

'*[Church services] are boring. Because it's generally for the older generation. Fair enough, if every young Christian went to church it could change.*'

'*I don't think church is very interesting for the young person. It's not really very lively. There's nothing special there for young people. I'd like to see more drama in church.*'

'*I think that's where you might get the generation gap, because I've known older people say, "How disgusting, we had*

*two electric guitars in the mass this morning and they were
playing this song and the music was banging out so loud." And I
think that's the generation gap, because the older people would
object to it, whereas all the younger generations prefer something
like that.'*

*'I'd love to go to a church that was more for young people... I
know it's better than some churches which have Holy
Communion Rite B or something like that—or a really boring
one, where they sing everything just like hymns.'*

The interviewer then asked: Do your Christian friends
think like you?

*'Most of them. Most of them don't go to church regularly.
Mostly they go once a month and go to CYFA instead.' (The
reference is to the Church Youth Fellowships Association.)*

This kind of comment was what we expected to hear. Our
inquiries suggested that it was less common than people
assume. Against it we can set the experience of Alan, who
felt that long extempore prayers were unhelpful for visitors.
He was able to make this point to an older member of the
congregation and was encouraged to take the issue to the
elders, the group of people in his church chosen to make
decisions for the church as a whole.

Again, Pat concluded a lengthy criticism of priests with a
positive statement about the congregation:

*'It's still the people. It's still that feeling of stood there in the
mass on a Sunday and all them people are there together and this
is the body of Christ.'*

Nick found his Methodist church unhelpful. Nevertheless
he was mature enough to consider his overall responsibilities:

*'But there's not many youngsters in the Methodist church
that I go to. They're mainly adults there. I'm going to try and
start going more often to the Methodist church because I've been
asked to by my mum. With that church being in Crosswell and
with us trying to evangelize in parts of Crosswell, then maybe
that's a good thing to do.'*

Paula was well aware of division in her church. But her
reaction seemed remarkably mature:

'*The friction that has come up from that recently has, you know, caused a lot of people to consider moving and the church is no longer flourishing. It is really becoming an effort. There is a group of Christians who really praise though and I hope I am one of them... Because we really need commitment in the church now, particularly while it is going through this sticky patch.*'

The stereotype claims that young people who don't get much out of church complain and leave. Wendy offered a different point of view:

'*I'm not getting a lot out of the services at the moment, but I might not be here much longer. So if I can be a bit of an encouragement while I'm still here...if there's any good left that I can do my church, I will, till I go to Poly.*'

Sally's remarks implied that the generation gap had been exaggerated:

'*[My church] covers all generations as well, from the young to the old. There's a big youth section of around my age that goes—and that's good because you can talk to each other about problems that you go through—and then there are the elder figures who help, you know, who you can go to for advice if you need help. They are the more mature Christians and that's good... I have been to churches where they think that young people have no place in the church, where you've got to reach the age of twenty-five before you're even considered to be a Christian and that really grinds on me.*'

These responses do not support the notion of the generation gap. They showed us young Christians who were not motivated by self-interest alone, who were aware of wider obligations and who, while recognizing the limitations of the local congregation, continued to express their commitment to it.

What do they appreciate about worship?

The questions we asked were open-ended enough to permit a wide range of answers. It is worth pointing out that the fact that some aspect of a church service was not mentioned does not mean that no one found it helpful. Our questions were likely to produce responses about the highlights of worship.

The sermon

That said, it is interesting to discover that a substantial number of young people mentioned the sermon as something helpful or significant. Thirteen out of sixty-two may not seem a particularly significant proportion. Nevertheless the myth of the teenage church-goer typically fastens on the sermon as that part of the service which is 'boring', 'irrelevant' and 'tedious'. Against this background it is worth reflecting on comments like these:

'Usually I get something out of the teaching. Whoever's preaching. That's the bit I usually really sit up and listen.'

'I like sermons that really bring home the message to you and make you...bring shivers to you really. I mean to make you understand God more from the sermon, to make you feel his power and that.'

'In church the most enjoyable part I find is the gospel and the sermon afterwards, because, you know, I like listening... listening to the passages. Especially if you've read it yourself. And then it's like the priest at the altar explaining it to you. You can understand it then and you get more out of it and it means more to you. And if you actually learn something...I mean if you've understood, even if it's only a tiny point...I mean learning a tiny point more every Sunday, then, you know, at the end of your life, you're not doing so bad.'

'OK, sometimes you get bored with the service and you go off. But the preacher says something and it'll strike you and you feel "Yeah!"'

The communion service

Not surprisingly the other element in worship which was frequently mentioned was the communion service, breaking of bread or mass. Just under half of the replies identified this as a significant aspect. Comments indicated that young people have a rich understanding of the eucharist and its theology.

Some concentrated on Christ's death and the experience of forgiveness:

'When I'm actually up there, what I usually think about is what Jesus has done for me. Sometimes I really feel the power of forgiveness.'

'I think it represents the fact that Jesus died for me. I know he died for everybody else as well. But that's very personal. And it's also a corporate thing and you're really all united by this fact.'

'Yes, we take it every Sunday morning in our church. You can take it lightly and just see it as...well, this is the bread and the wine. But you know, it's a really significant thing if you take it seriously because it's the one thing... Jesus came and died and that helps us to remember it and remember why he did it.'

'Communion...yes, I enjoy that, taking the bread and the ribena wine, yes, so that's important. It's sort of remembering Jesus died for you. Well, it's like if you had an interview for a job...and you got the job. Once you'd got the job you'd forget about the interview. But it's not like that because you're always told that Jesus died for you on the cross and that's important to remember... I mean to send your son or your daughter to death when people spat on him and hated him, that would take great love, so I think it's very important.'

Others stressed the unity of Christians which the service expressed:

'It's important because it brings everybody together.'

'When you go to communion, you're all together, which is togetherness, and, you see, you also feel more like you are with Jesus.'

'I think it's marvellous how these people love God and I think there's something holy, something very beautiful about people just going forward. It means so much to a lot of people.'

For others it is a time for feeding on Christ, rejoicing in his presence and drawing strength and life for the week ahead:

'The communion is special. It's a time I feel I can draw closest

to Christ and feel one and the same… I'm in him and he's in me, sort of thing.'

'You eat the bread and drink the wine and you can feel it going down you. It's lovely. Such a joy follows it and a peace and it's lovely.'

'The actual taking of bread and wine…sort of symbolizes Jesus' life.'

'I don't really like churches who make a very solemn do out of it because I know it's about remembering he died for us, but although he died for us, it's also a very joyous occasion because he gave us eternal life, you know…'

'It's no longer I that live but Christ that lives in me.'

'In communion that bread that I take, I take as a symbol of God giving strength to me. It strengthens me for all the things I have to do during the week. And the blood I take to be a symbol of washing one right the way through. This is my own personal view.'

It was fascinating to listen to Mark trying to express his own sense that the rite marks more than an act of remembrance:

'I think as I'm actually receiving the bread and the wine, there are…it usually happens there…I am extremely vague—and this is more probably vague than anything else where I've used the word "vague" previously—but in some vague way…in some way that I can't put into words at all…it's more than remembering…er…the Last Supper and Jesus. I can't say in what way but it's just that very slight hint of it being more.'

There was general agreement that the communion service was important and valuable. In the main, young people did not expect to be entertained by the service. They recognized that they might have to work at their participation:

'But when it's interesting and it's a good mass for you, you come out and you feel like you've accomplished something and you've learnt something by it.'

'I am a regular attender at church and the eucharist seems the most significant part of the mass to me. I'm not just thinking about the receiving of communion but the whole ceremony of the eucharist.'

87

And just occasionally they seem to have caught the sense of standing within a long tradition and recognizing the age-old continuity of Christendom:

'Through all those thousands of years it's been passed down. And that tradition is still alive and still going strong. And that's really a great thing. We have it every week in our church.'

This emphasis on the sermon and the communion service reflects the responses of the young people. But it would be misleading to give the impression that this was all that they found helpful or significant. A wide range of other aspects of worship was also mentioned. Taken together they do not give the impression of a generation at odds with the institutional church:

The Peace, the general confession, services of sorrow and reconciliation, novenas, open prayer, the stations of the cross, the music group, 'world-wide' prayers, the collect for purity, the Christmas midnight mass, a cross suspended above the altar, testimonies, the silence and peace of a cathedral, the dignity and order of the liturgy, dancing, the band, guitars, clapping, an intimate service in a side chapel, 'a time of ministry', old churches, family services.

This list suggests that many aspects of church life can enable young people to experience a deeper side of their faith. Indeed this is what we should expect. A more fruitful line of inquiry might be to turn away from the furniture, the scenery and the format and to concentrate on the spirit of worship. What did young people find helpful and unhelpful about the manner in which they experienced worship?

The spirit of worship

This is an elusive idea and it becomes especially difficult to make generalizations that are true for all the church denominations. Young people imbibe the traditions of their church very efficiently. What counts as 'freedom' or 'participation' will vary according to the normal style of worship. In an evangelical or charismatic church the people who worship may appreciate the freedom they have in such a setting to take part in the worship. In a church that has a set liturgy to be followed in all its services, a similar level of freedom may only be found at special events, such as a houseparty. However, in spite of the difficulties involved in trying to see similarities and differences, we felt that the young people together identified four distinct features of meaningful worship.

Involvement

Nine of the young people we spoke to commented unfavourably on unnecessarily long prayers or sermons or, in the case of Catholics, 'masses that ramble on a bit'. It is possible that this kind of comment merely reflects the attention-span of young people today. It is more likely, however, that it is not the length that is the substance of the objection so much as the feeling that they are no longer being involved in what is going on. Hence Beth's observation: 'It's very much the vicar at the front of the congregation whereas I like something where we're all brought together.'

In similar vein, Ruth, a very intelligent and talented seventeen-year-old observed:

'*There doesn't seem to be any real interaction. There's just the vicar at the front. He's speaking and the congregation are the other way... The vicar has his little bit, then we have our response and they don't seem to interact.*'

Encouraging a sense of involvement may be more difficult in some forms of service than others. It is notable that the teenagers who attended the more participatory worship of the Free Evangelical and house-church kind often commented on the freedom which they had to 'worship God in your own way'.

'*Somebody will say, "I'll take the meeting tonight. I've got this word." So they'll read it and then they'll ask, "What do you think, George?" and he'll say what he thinks and then the whole lot of us will get into a discussion.*'

'I think you should let God know how you feel...not just by praying but by showing it, dancing and singing with all your heart and just letting him know, and having good fun at the same time.'

'At our church we have songs and then use single sentence prayers like "I worship you because..." and other people sometimes put into words what you think. And then, "I thank you because..." And you really sort of say them yourself... "...because You, Lord, are Creator." And you really centre on who he is. That helps as well.'

This desire for feeling involved, sometimes expressed as 'freedom' to worship and 'participation', 'interaction' or 'sharing', was mentioned by twenty-five of those we spoke to. It clearly represented a deep desire to feel personally involved in what was going on. It is one of the reasons why music and singing are so frequently cited as vital to 'good worship'. In churches where a set liturgy is used, it is harder for members of the congregation to join in. In these settings, the desire for involvement surfaced in the enthusiastic description of worship at houseparties or youth fellowships.

Sincerity

Not unreasonably the young Christians we spoke to expected those who were engaged in the conduct of worship to be sincere. In many cases they were probably over-critical of what they perceived as insincerity, no doubt unfairly castigating ministers for faults which they were struggling hard to eradicate. However, there was no doubt that they reserved some of their harshest comments for the leader who was 'merely going through the motions', for whom the service was 'just a formality' or who, in some other way, was falling short.

'At the Pentecostal church before the evening service, we've got a kind of warm-up session where we sing choruses and the person who leads it—well, different ones lead it but they tend to be from a certain clique—and you get the same people doing it and they tend to say much the same thing every time. It's the

links that annoy me, not the choruses. We tend to have the same links and the same choruses. But it's annoying when you hear these platitudes. It's a sort of ritual in itself, except that it doesn't admit to being liturgy, which is worse, in a way.'

'I didn't feel that the preacher...he didn't have something about him. I know you shouldn't judge but when somebody preaches you can tell whether he's had an experience of something, you know.'

'Priests annoy me. Priests have given up their life to be priests and their main function is, you know, celebrate the mass, right? And that's their main function and they've given up their whole life for that. They've given up marriage, they've given up a normal life. And...they don't make any attempt to make it special. They just come in and they do it... They're terrified of giving you themselves. All they ever give you is Father Smith, Father, Father, Father. They never give you the person they are, you see. And the priest's role is a sacrificial role. They've given themselves up and they don't. They take it back again.'

Here Pat was clearly speaking out of deep personal resentment and her comment represents one of the harshest criticisms of what she saw as clerical hypocrisy. In total, eight of our eleven Catholic respondents made a negative comment about worship which appeared to be 'just a job', something 'to be rushed through', a 'routine mass'. Seven of the twenty-five teenagers from free churches criticized what they saw as the empty formalism and barren repetition of the Anglican liturgy. Whether or not these comments were fair, they nevertheless showed how those who made them were thinking.

Community

Churches claim to be part of the body of Christ—meaning that church members are Christ's representatives on earth. With typical idealism young Christians expect them to be so in a very practical way. They hoped for a sense of belonging to a community. They wanted to experience warmth and friendliness from other members.

91

'I never used to look forward to church at all—it was something I had a commitment to do on Sundays. But now I can't wait. And I enjoy the fellowship as well. There's so much love in that place. Everybody just loves everybody else. Everybody there is so genuine.'

Tom discovered this kind of intimacy in worship when a new priest came to the nine-o'clock mass.

'He said, "You must all come up to the front, all gather round the altar." And we said the mass together and then he handed the communion out and it was dead warm and far closer and much better than them all spread around the church, and I enjoyed that.'

'People come together, and witness together, and choose to be together to say "We are standing together to support." Belonging…and so on.'

'The feeling of togetherness. We are all there, you know, the people who believe, and there's the most remarkable feeling and spirit. Everyone really loves one another. And we're all that is together, really praising God, really thanking him and it really comes out.'

It is clear that these young Christians were responsive to this sense of unity in the Spirit that comes from sharing the same beliefs and knowing the same God. Some of the negative comments we received came from experiences where they believed it had been suppressed. For example, a Catholic boy was angry that a priest had shut young children away in the creche. An Anglican girl said that she felt 'so unwelcome' in a church in Yeovil, 'Everybody would walk away on you; it was as if you were a shadow.' Another girl sensed that she was not valued as part of a family but was seen as so much 'pew fodder':

'If I haven't been for a couple of weeks or a month and I came to a particular sermon, or this or that, the vicar now won't say, "Oh, it's nice to see you. I'm glad to see you. How've you been?" and that. He'll say, "Where have you been? Why have you come today and not every other Sunday?"'

Atmosphere

It is very difficult to define this term. At its worst it might be taken to refer just to services which resemble concerts or entertainments. Certainly the 'celebration' was valued by young Christians and many of them mentioned large scale para-church events such as the Dales Bible Week, Greenbelt, and the Methodist Association of Youth Clubs weekends. One asked wistfully why her church was not like Lourdes. It would be unreasonable to demand that the weekly worship of the local congregation should match the multi-media, semi-professional, national 'youth events'. But this is not all that young people were pointing to when they said that they appreciated 'atmosphere'.

Elusive though the term may be, 'atmosphere' seems to point towards a sense that something worthwhile is going on. Young people mentioned 'life' in the service and spoke about being 'uplifted'.

'And in St John's there's a sort of very good atmosphere that I feel. It's very hard to put into words again but I feel the atmosphere, and I suppose the frame of mind that you're in as well. But I suppose the general atmosphere I find, as being...there's something about it...'

Obviously, this quality is more easily recognized than defined. It is mediated through context and setting but not reducible to these. The young people seemed to attribute it to a combination of whole-heartedness in the worshippers and the activity of God. So the paraphernalia of worship were often cited—music, singing, dancing, silence—but this reference was immediately qualified by a comment about the spiritual dimension. The comments reveal an intensity of spiritual experience that might seem intimidating to someone who has not been through it.

'I don't think there's anything more lovely than when the music's playing on its own and somebody's singing in the Spirit, because I can close my eyes and imagine...imagine angels. I can just feel angels around me. That might seem a bit silly but I can.'

'You can't drift away. You've got your eyes on him [the preacher] all the time. And you're listening to him and agreeing with him and you're able to agree. You can shout out and agree.'

'I'd describe the worship of our present church as excitable, exciting. It's sort of pentecostal and charismatic. It's always very joyful and usually quite loud. People are usually taken up with it.'

These excerpts may give the impression that 'atmosphere' is only to be found in unstructured, charismatic worship of a rather dramatic kind. 'Life' was not described as just a matter of free expression and powerful demonstrations of God's presence.

'Of the places I found, I found the cathedral was really nice because it was somewhere where I could think about my faith...think about what I was feeling and...it's much quieter usually and... I suppose quite freely isolated.'

Our conclusion was that young people recognized whole-hearted, sincere worship when they encountered it and responded positively. However, it may seem a tall order to ask that every service be 'special', 'something of an occasion' and this is probably why worship at youth fellowships and weekend houseparties were so often recalled. Twenty-five of our sample mentioned such para-church organizations or events. As we have already indicated, for most they were not a substitute for church but a valuable complement to it. In so far as involvement, community and atmosphere are more easily obtained on these occasions, we can understand why they figured so prominently in young Christians' replies.

'We once went to a Peace Sunday and it was in the cathedral and there were loads of young people there. It was really a youth mass and we all prayed for peace throughout the world. Then afterwards all the youth went into the Irish centre. That's next door and we had discussions and talks and that.'

'The communion that is held at the end of the week is usually moving and very lively.'

'At the Dales...this special prayer with six thousand people

and just being able to get properly roused... There was, how shall I put it, a "special atmosphere".'

'I see the small group of friends that I meet to pray with as being the church. I find a comparison in the early church where a group of Christians used to meet together to pray and have communion and then they used to go to the temple and all sit together. I see that as being really important.'

The discipline of worship

This final section explores the area of preparing for worship. We wanted to know how far young Christians recognized that they had an obligation to prepare for worship, how far they expected to be roused, stimulated, moved or enlightened by others. Worship in consumerist terms is all a matter of getting something out of it. In Christian theology worship is precisely the opposite. It has no extrinsic, utilitarian value.

This point was accepted by Mandy:

'My mum keeps telling me, "It's not what you can get out of it but what you can put in." I keep telling myself that, but I still find church very boring... I wish I didn't find it boring.'

Thirty-six young people spoke of preparing themselves in some way for worship. In this they showed a remarkably high level of responsibility. Attendance at worship laid clear obligations on them. Their own demands for sincerity in the leader were matched by their desire to come into God's presence with a similar integrity.

Some expressed this serious intent as trying to open themselves to God:

'What I look for most is what God, Jesus, is going to teach us. Even though that's sometimes a bit heavy going.'

'Therefore I feel that it's most important that you be quiet before the Lord...that you can really sense him.'

'I'm bearing in mind when I go in that what's going to happen will be something new to me, and what is going to happen will be something I'm going to enjoy, because I'm expecting things to happen.'

'I just remind myself that church isn't a club. It's not CYFA. It's actually a place where people meet to worship in fellowship with God, and I have to remember I'm going there to meet God.'

'I just try to open up to see what the Lord has to say to us, 'cos what I might want to be taught at the time isn't necessarily what Jesus wants to teach us.'

Others took care to set themselves right with God and others before participating.

'I feel that most of all at communion because you've got everything sorted out, hopefully, beforehand and you can go up there and say, "I want to be a part of you and be like you." Sometimes if I'm not able to see the person [I need to sort things out with] in church before I take communion, I don't go up until I've talked to the person.'

'To clear myself of all sins, I like to go back over the past week, see where I've sinned, say sorry for it, and if there's anyone I'm on bad terms with, I like to say sorry to them and make it up with them.'

'Sometimes I won't go to communion if I've got something on my mind, because communion means a union with people and with God.'

'There's nothing we can hide, either feeling or what we've done or what we are, from him and there's no use trying to hide it. The sooner we realize that the better.'

For some the question of active participation was important. They clearly felt that they ought not to remain spectators or passengers and that they had an obligation to offer something of themselves in worship.

'Raising of hands as well. That is something else I'd like to do. I think it's just something when you're singing—quiet songs— and the Holy Spirit is there, then it is so natural for some people to put their hands up in the air.'

'What I'm trying to do now, every week when I go to church, is to sort of dedicate part of the service to a certain group of people or to a certain friend. And last week it was to my family.'

'I would want to participate whenever possible. I wouldn't say I have the gift of tongues but I would say I am used in the gift of tongues.'

Many commented on the importance of concentrating on what was being said or sung and on not letting the mind wander:

'If I really understood the importance of it, then I wouldn't take communion when I wasn't really thinking about it. If I understood in my heart I wouldn't just go through the motions.'

'I try to make a conscious effort and concentrate on the prayer for transformation and the communion itself. I try to force myself to cut myself off from everything else I'm doing, so I can concentrate particularly on the part of the mass itself.'

'I tend to turn my eyes away from myself and focus on Jesus. I find the best way to do this is to actually look up at Jesus on the cross in the stained glass-window behind the altar.'

'Well, I try to think why I'm actually there. Because when I'm listening to the homily, without a doubt my mind's not on the mass (and I don't think quite a few people's are) and I feel as if I've wasted my time at the mass because I haven't really been there.'

The folk myth of the bored teenager who is interested only in being entertained in church and despises the older members of the congregation needs drastic modification in the light of all these comments. This group of young Christians demonstrated remarkable levels of commitment to their local churches. They also seemed to be fully aware of what worship required of them and, for the most part, they were making serious and mature attempts to meet those demands.

References

[1]Bernice Martin and Ronald Pluck, *Young People's Beliefs*, General Synod Board of Education, 1976, p.16.

[2]*op. cit.*, p.17.

[3]*op. cit.*, p.13.

8
Talking to God

I try to start off by thinking the day through and thinking of all the things I want to thank God for.

God's my friend but he's also my father and I'm going to talk to him as a father.

I feel real peaceful even though sometimes my insides are all jumping with excitement.

That time when prayer is not answered, and you pass it off, yeah, yeah. You pass it off.

Prayer is a peculiar activity at the best of times. To the unbeliever it looks like auto-suggestion or even the most appalling self-deception. Yet in orthodox Christian teaching prayer is the essence of the life of faith. All traditions and denominations stress that the key to Christian maturity lies in a regular and disciplined devotional life.

At the same time prayer is also the place where the shoe pinches most. Some views of prayer seem to emphasize its instrumental function, as if it were a conveniently labour-saving way of getting things done. This can lead to a quietism which fails to grapple with problems or to a form of double-think which sees 'answers to prayer' in the most unconvincing incidents. At its worst it may produce a consumerism which uses God and calls on him just to bail you out of a crisis.

Prayer is also an area of Christian living where the gap between profession and practice can be especially wide. The rhetoric of Christian groups stresses the vital importance of prayer and can make it very difficult for members to express doubts or admit to failures. Yet despite all the talk of a 'friendship with God' through prayer, the uncompromising fact remains that God is invisible and does not always respond as clearly or audibly as other friends. Prayer may be the place of the deepest fulfilment, the encounter from which the life of faith draws all its meaning and power, or it may be the situation in which the Christian feels most foolish.

We were interested to see how young teenaged Christians handled these issues. We asked them how much they prayed, when, where and how, and what they thought was going on when they were doing so. We also wanted to know how far they saw prayer as the means to a relationship with God. And, of course, we were interested in any other ways in which they tried to develop their spirituality. In all this we were aware that we were entirely dependent on the answers they gave us. However, we think that their comments represent genuine conviction and a fair description of their practice, even though we are aware of the possibility of self-deception and the desire to impress in such a crucial area of the Christian life.

Discipline

How disciplined and systematic does the life of prayer need to be? The interview material makes it clear that the majority of young people had received the message that daily 'quiet times', when the individual spends time alone reading the Bible, meditating and praying, were the heart of the business. Most claimed to pray regularly and believed that it was important to do so. About two thirds of our sample tried to organize this on a daily pattern. Many expressed the view that it was best to try to find time in the morning before breakfast but in practice it was easier to pray at the end of the day. About a dozen had managed to maintain morning prayer times, though with many admissions of failure. The morning was a time of 'chaos', 'total panic', when you felt 'shattered'. Half the group had their major or only formal time of prayer in the evening. A sample of the answers will give the flavour of the whole:

'*Yes, I pray regularly every night and of course I pray at church as well.*'

'*I try and have a quiet time. It's usually before I go to sleep. I used to try and have a quiet time in the morning, but it was too much. That was a better time really because you usually feel you're starting the day off right. But now it tends to be after you've done a load of work and I go up to my room and have about half an hour then.*'

'*I try to pray regularly, before I go to bed, and very briefly before I get up in a morning. The time varies from three to four minutes to half an hour.*'

'*Well, I try to set aside a quiet time every morning. I get up earlier. I get up at seven. I start about half past and I finish about quarter past...twenty past eight, and then I go to school. I prefer the morning because I think I'm a morning person rather than an evening person.*'

To be fair, few were quite as well organized as this girl. Many spoke of prayer as 'difficult': 'it slips my mind'; 'I break the Catholic rules'; 'it depends on my mood'; ' my mind wanders'; 'I'm off and on'. And clearly some of the young people were locked into the kind of struggle to achieve a discipline of time which is familiar to the adult churchgoer:

'*I try to make it often but it tends to become very patchy, you know. I'll just be coming to a point where it is...where I've got it going in a good routine and then I'll find that it slips away and I'll try and put aside an extra half hour in the morning so I can be sure to fit it in. But you find it gets filled in in some other way, and I really have to push myself to get back into the routine again.*'

'*I think as well that I get too tired, it's... I mean last night I was lying in bed and I was thinking about everything I should have been praying for and I was just gradually drifting off to sleep and waking up and saying, "You haven't finished yet." I*'

100

don't do it every morning but I would like to get into the habit of it more. I will one day. I try to make up for it during the day.'

'They say you should do it in the morning but I like to sleep and I get up at 7.15... I'm usually rushing for the bus at that time, so I've never really got time in the morning. When I come back from work, I usually go for a run and then have tea... Usually I do it on a night, which is the worst time to do it, and that's how I come to miss it, 'cos you're tired and in bed.'

They would have envied sixteen-year-old Nick who was untroubled by such difficulties:

'No, I don't find it difficult to pray regularly. It doesn't take much to pray. You could just lie in bed and pray. I've been praying for as long as I can remember.'

There was evidence of careful teaching about what 'ought' to go on within the prayer time. Jill gave us one of the more organized and systematic versions:

'I try to start off by thinking the day through and thinking of all the things I want to thank God for. And then I've usually got to get the things I'm sorry for off quickly, otherwise they prey on my mind and I can't think of much else. Some days though, I think through the day and I can't think of anything specially that I want to say sorry for, and then I know there must be thousands of things I've done that I should be feeling guilty about. I feel bad when it's just, "Dear God, sorry for all the things I did wrong today." 'Cos I know I should be thinking out the individual things so I can't do them next time. Sometimes I find that really hard to do and sometimes they all come bubbling to the forefront and I can apologize for them. After I've done that it'll be getting on to, "How should I approach such and such?" and "I'm really concerned for X and Y. Should I be reaching out to them or just keeping a pace away and keeping an eye on them?" Or just general conversation about things that I feel I need help with or thanking him or praying for details that people have need for prayer with, and things like that.'

All this is very structured and self-conscious. A substantial group wanted to insist on greater freedom and spontaneity. In some of the responses one detected the voice of adolescent independence, a disinclination to be told how to regulate what should be a matter of instant access and personal freedom.

'No I don't pray regularly. That doesn't work for me. Nothing regular like that helps me at all. I pray when I want to pray or when I need to. Really I know that sounds a bit wrong... You can pray even when you're not even realizing that you're praying... And nobody can force you to pray, you know. If you were brought up in a Christian family and they got you to sit down at seven o'clock that night and got you to pray, your mind could be on something else, but they wouldn't know.'

'People don't have to pray, you know.'

'I pray just when I feel like it really.'

'I try to pray often but I only pray when I think of it... I just do it when I need to.'

'I don't sort of get on my knees, or whatever, at a special time. I mean I usually pray in the bath or the shower or when I'm jogging along or running to catch the bus. I pray when I need to pray... I need to talk to God, say, when I'm waiting for the bus. You have no one else to talk to in the shower. I might sing aloud. Singing a nice song, I count that as praying. I might say, "Well, God, I hope I'll be all right today. Keep me out of trouble today before I go."'

Whatever the merits of this kind of free and easy, uninhibited approach to God, it runs the risk of collapsing into pure self-indulgence. God is permanently on tap, instantly available in the way a radio station can be picked up and put down according to the mood of the moment. A different kind of cry for freedom from the 'system' comes from Penny:

'A lot of meetings we've had on prayer, they say the first thing you have to do is praise, then you have to thank God for all the things that have happened through the week, then you have to ask forgiveness for all the things you've done wrong, and then you have to ask for other people, and then you have to ask for yourself. But I don't do that at all. When I tell people that I don't follow the rule, they say I should, because this is what

*ordinary Christians do, and I say, "No, God's my friend but
he's also my father and I'm going to talk to him like a father."
So I tell him how I feel usually, or sometimes I feel words are just
useless and so limited, so I just stay quiet and listen to my heart
and I just let him listen to all the things that are going on in my
head.'*

The effect of prayer

It is extremely difficult to formulate a theory of prayer which
does not lead into incoherence. Many adult Christians would
shrink from having to give an account of what they thought
they were doing when they prayed. The young people we
spoke to found it no easier. Nevertheless, we were able to
discern some assumptions and understandings of prayer
which seemed to underpin the practice.

There was near-universal agreement that prayer was some
kind of communication with God. This was variously
expressed as 'making contact', 'a two-way conversation', 'a
dialogue', 'companionship', 'talking to a friend', 'having a
mate', 'a channel', 'a phone-call', 'a link'.

*'When you say your prayers you've just got a special link,
and until you cross yourself and say Amen that link never goes.
It's always there continuously.'*

*'Nobody knows what's inside you, only God can really
understand you. And it's important that he can pick out how to
help you. Sometimes you can just say prayers, you know, not
formal prayers, but just talking to God as though you're
speaking to him.'*

Only one reply compared God to a 'mighty king' to whom
'his subjects' come in humility. Most saw God as an instantly
accessible friend in whom to confide. Typically he was close
and could be spoken to in intimate terms. He was interested in
every aspect of life, even the most trivial.

*'He knows what I'm going through and he's getting really
close to me and empathizing with everything I'm thinking.'*

Whereas some of the young people expressed doubts about

103

answers to prayers in the shape of external, specific events, there appeared to be no doubt in their minds that God listens. He hears the cry of his children.

'I think he listens. I know he's listening. And I think he's longing to hear me pray. I don't hear him talk back to me or anything, but I know he's listening to me. I know I talk absolute nonsense to him at times but I know he'll always listen.'

'I imagine him to be listening. If my mind wanders sometimes I think he's been sitting there and saying, "Come on, Mary." It's like me sitting next to you and suddenly talking about something totally irrelevant to what you've asked me and ignoring you. And I would have to apologize to you and apologize to Jesus and say, "Thanks for bringing me back to consciousness. I'm really sorry. My mind wandered." And I presume he's there and listening.'

Within this general understanding of the prayer situation three different aspects might be stressed, though these were not seen as mutually exclusive.

First, there were those replies which emphasized the quiet place, 'the still point in the turning world'. Praying was a way of encountering God and receiving his peace. It was a way of 'being with God', rather than engaging in a transaction.

'As soon as I enter into prayer there's a peace there. Sometimes I can't find words and I find that passage...that says, "The Spirit is always groaning in words that we cannot understand." I find that very helpful.'

'That helps you really because it brings you out of yourself, because sometimes you need to be on your own, and sometimes even if you only sit and think, if you just collect your thoughts together and talk, it really seems to help because sometimes you can't get that relationship with other people... You need the kind of relationship you can find with God, and it's special because he understands you. Perhaps he's the only person who really does.'

'I feel real peaceful even though sometimes my insides are all jumping with excitement... I feel really special and really loved as well.'

104

'Part of my prayers is being still.'

Second, some concentrated on the opportunity of 'off-loading' the problems of the day. In prayer you could fully and honestly express your feelings. There was considerable value in being able to share one's innermost thoughts with a truly understanding and confidential friend.

'[Prayer] is the only way in which you can express your fear, your thoughts and your feelings and things. Especially if you're scared about something. And sometimes that's the only way you can get that fear out.'

'If you want God to know you, God must know you for the sort of person you are.'

'Praying for me is just really a way of asking him what I've been doing and why this or that has happened and what are you going to do, and things like that.'

'It may be asking him what he's doing, you know, doing something to me for.'

Third, prayer might be seen as the place where illumination could be found. It might be the means to greater self-awareness, deeper understanding of oneself and, often through scripture, of light on difficult areas of life.

'I also pray...that's sort of thanking God for things and for revealing to me exactly how I feel and why.'

'I think of it as a new light that I'd never thought of before. I think that's God answering, saying, "You can't think of it like this. It makes a lot more sense if you think of it like that."'

God's response

We were interested in whether young Christians held any well thought out view of prayer as a way of asking for things. Did they see any difficulties with this approach? Did they understand prayer in any way as 'work'? Did their concept of prayer relate it to God's activity in the world? Did prayer 'make a difference' and, if so, how?

The answers show that, for them, prayer is not just a matter of navel gazing. It was expected to have identifiable effects, though it was accepted that these might not be blindingly obvious, would often be ambiguous and would frequently have to be accepted on faith. But the fact that one girl had 'a massive prayer list' and that several emphasized that prayer must be 'believing', 'not selfish' and was 'like asking someone for a favour' show the beginnings of a doctrine of how to ask for things in prayer. But as Mandy said, 'Things just seem to happen so I assume God is working but how, I'm not yet sure. I'll wait till I get up there to ask him.'

Prayer certainly was a source of personal spiritual power. Without it one would not have the strength to help oneself or other people. In this way prayer might affect the way things were.

'I begin to see for myself that it really helps you through the day and you can go through feeling happy.'

Second, prayer could be seen as releasing something into the situation, removing a blockage to divine power, 'allowing' God to act in people who did not acknowledge his existence.

'In a sense it is my contribution in letting the Lord notice you more, because you've been put in my prayer... If I pray for someone who I know doesn't pray, I know the Lord would take special care of that person because of me.'

'I feel I'm holding up the situation to God and saying, "You're in control now." I'm bringing him into that situation.'

There were those who were prepared to go further even than the notion of releasing power. Sometimes we were able to ask if certain events would only occur if someone had prayed. Was God in any sense prepared deliberately to limit himself to human prayers?

'It almost seems as if the Lord is saying, "Unless you pray, I won't..." I just think that maybe the Lord depends on us to pray to him. And therefore he is depending totally on us. We have free will. We can choose whether to pray or not.'

The interviewer then asked, 'Are there things that happen that wouldn't have happened if you hadn't prayed?' Kathy replied with feeling:

'*Yes, yes, time and time again. But first, let me just say, there was this girl when I—how guilty I still feel—this girl said, "I've got my driving test." "Don't worry, I'll pray for you," I said. And I didn't and she failed. For all I know, if I'd have prayed...*'

It was fascinating to listen to Paula grappling with an idea with which she had never before been confronted:

'*I've never been asked that one! I believe God does what is right... We wouldn't know, would we?*'

The interviewer asked, 'What is the point of praying for somebody else?'

'*It shows you know the need is there... But then you know that anyway, don't you? He knows the need is there... So it shows you know the need is there.*'

When pressed to explain, she admitted:

'*I don't know. That's a difficult question. You've put me on the spot.*'

The interviewer persisted: 'You are praying for a non-Christian friend... How do you see that situation?' Paula replied:

'*There's God, there's your friend and there's you. God knows your attitude towards it...a particular situation and... Well, he knows that anyway, doesn't he? Ah! Right! He knows that you are willing to let something work through you and he will use your willingness to ease the situation.*'

What to pray for?

The view of God as an ever-present friend implies that every aspect of life, no matter how mundane, may be the subject of prayer. The list of topics contained very few surprises. For example, it will come as no shock to learn that young Christians prayed about their school work and especially the outcome of examinations. One boy said, 'Come on, God, are you going to get me my A's?' Another said that her prayer time went up hundred per cent during the pre-exam revision period. They also prayed to be kept safe, 'out of trouble'.

'Get me out of this,' was a common thought, however expressed. In addition they prayed for their friends, particularly those who were not Christians—that they might come to faith—and for those who were ill or 'going through a rough time'.

The world of the teenager may seem a very restricted one. They were concerned with examinations, with broken relationships, driving tests, friends who dabbled with drugs or were 'going off the rails', with a peer group which evidenced little interest in the faith but contained some who might be 'won for Christ'. It is arguable that their prayers were no more domestic than those of most adult Christians. Nevertheless the point ought still to be made that we found no example of prayer for wider issues, no petitions for governments or leaders, no concern for national, political or global affairs.

Within the range of topics for which they did pray, however, they were able to cite numerous examples of answers to prayer. For example, Barry felt ill but suddenly recovered only to discover later in the day that his friend had been praying for him. Richard had been going through a difficult time but after David had prayed 'for a long time', 'things smoothed out for him'. Linda, the most hostile member of the class and the one who swore the most, became a Christian. The car with a near empty tank continued for another thirty miles. Tickets for the film *The Cross and the Switchblade* were going badly until the Christian group prayed and then sales rose. Paul was feeling drowsy while driving on the motorway but stopped, prayed and acquired renewed alertness and the ability to concentrate.

It is not our concern to argue whether these really are answers to prayer or examples of wishful thinking. What they do reveal is a doctrine of prayer and a doctrine of God which is being worked out 'on the hoof' as it were. God is involved in every aspect of one's life. He may be prayed to about any matter, large or trivial. The teenager who spoke about praying on the toilet ('it's so peaceful there') demonstrates the unembarrassed and natural way in which God is brought into the everyday.

Most of what the young Christians said was positive and optimistic. Prayer was important, 'vital' even. God listened and answered. He showed himself actively concerned in their everyday concerns and hopes. On the whole they were untroubled by philosophical problems to do with prayer, preferring to engage in the practice and leave the outcome to God. Two replies showed that there were problems of imagining how God could deal with 'thousands and thousands of requests at once' but for most, the difficulty of the harrassed switchboard operator and the in-coming calls could be easily brought beneath an adequate doctrine of the nature of God. It simply was not a problem.

Prayer and the inner life

Occasionally, however, we were able to hear a different voice. Here the questionings arose from the practice of prayer. It was more a problem of plausibility. Was the whole business of prayer just a form of self-comfort?

'I can't really say with the reality of the day and all this science and technology and learning all about stuff that happens in the physics and chemistry laboratories with evidence... I'm going home and I'm praying to this God in the sky and I think it's a bit sort of stupid.'

'I've got to be honest with you. You have got to believe it happened but not really the way I wanted it to. "The Lord works in a mysterious way." It's a good quote, isn't it? That time when prayer is not answered, and you pass it off, yeah, yeah. You pass it off.'

'I try and really believe in it as much as I can. And I try and sometimes I stop and listen and wait and see if anything happens and I try not to call myself silly sometimes when I'm praying.'

'I've never known God to talk to me yet. I know he's there. Maybe one day. I hope so. I wouldn't mind him talking to me. If he has, I don't know about it.'

'It's not being able to see him. You talk to him but he doesn't actually talk to you back in a voice. Sometimes you can sort of say to yourself, "Well, I don't think you've heard me at all, so why don't you show me something?" The biggest thing is not being able to have a conversation with him half the time. It seems to be only one way most of the time, because you're talking and he's not saying a lot.'

We sense the doubt and the wistful desire to have more evidence. Like many adult Christians, these young people were struggling with aspects of their faith that seemed confusing.

At the other extreme were those whose experience of God in prayer was almost too real. Some were engaged in struggle, in living through a robust relationship with God, almost wanting to run away from the relationship and its responsibilities. There is very little notion of the consumerist in these excerpts:

'Generally when you're feeling sorry for yourself, it's because he's given you a good hiding... I could say that when I went to college I didn't stick in. I got a good hiding from him for what I'd done. "Ee, what have I done?" You know. "Sorry, Lord." And I learned the hard way. He doesn't give you a clip on the ear for nothing.'

'To actually sit down and do the one-to-one sort of prayer...it frightens me because I always feel that when you pray like that, you always put yourself at risk. Because you're opening yourself to something that has a really wicked sense of humour and it's sort of scary. It's sort of...you're probably going to come off with something else you've got to do... I'll say hello every now and again and "I still know you're there" sort of thing. "But I don't want to talk to you because that's a bit too risky." He might say, "I want you to be an enclosed nun." "I want you to renounce this." "I don't think you're doing this right."'

It would be unfair to end the discussion at this point, however. For some of the young people, prayer, even petitionary prayer, was a way of being with God, a way of developing a relationship with him. The three examples which conclude the chapter seemed to us to show how prayer could be part of a deepening spirituality.

The first concerns someone with a longstanding and seriously debilitating illness. He had prayed to be healed on many occasions and after one morning service in particular had been reduced to tears by what seemed to be the hopelessness of his case. Nevertheless he was convinced that he was being healed gradually. How would he reply to the hard questions about the effectiveness of prayer?

'First I'd ask them why they'd asked me. If anybody is to ask the question it should be me. Because it's me and not them. If I get bothered about it, then it's up to me to ask and not for anyone else to use it as an excuse for whatever they're trying to persuade me. I would then say if this is what the Lord wants to do, then it's fine with me. One thing I'm convinced it's not: that it's because of something that parents, relatives or myself had done. Because there is evil in the world, because of Adam... And the next thing is to bring glory to God's name when I am healed in front of however many people are going to be there.'

The second is a sensitive account of how prayer and action can together be part of co-operating with God in the wider work of salvation.

'Last year I worked in a tracking centre with horses, because I love horses. Now there's a caravan site near and there was a tiny little boy; he was gorgeous. He was with his family and he was backward. He was very slow... He had very big eyes and he kept looking at me and he was obviously terrified at the animals... Now there was a little pony called Lightning, a little Shetland pony. Really sweet. He was quiet and I knew it wouldn't move and I knew it wouldn't muck about, so I said, "Come on, come and see the pony," but he wouldn't. Anyway, during the night, in the evening, I was praying and I thought about him. The Lord sort of put it into my mind. So I thought, oh, right, I'll pray about this... Anyway, I prayed, went to bed, went to sleep, woke up next morning, got the horses into the yard. There were obviously masses of horses and I could see why he was afraid. I mean, if you're this high and the horses are up here

111

somewhere, it must be really frightening. Anyway, his parents brought him along, and he looked at me like this and I said, "Come on, come on." I took his hand and took him over to the pony. So I said, "Come on, I'll put you on the back of the horse." Now the last time I suggested that, he had a fit and screamed, so I picked him up and put him on the horse and he sat there and loved it, stroked him. It was great. I was all choked up and said, "Oh, praise the Lord, that's great." And his father said, "Well, he has a learning problem, he's slightly backward; but what you've done is marvellous. Bless you. Bless you." And as soon as he said that, I thought, "Yes, it is a blessing." Someone so little, obviously terrified and with problems anyway. Now happy and confident. Oh that was good.'

Andy's experience is interesting because, through it, he seems to have come to an understanding of prayer as being open to the grace of God rather than asking for things. He had been asked to pray for a friend who was 'going off to be a nun' but was troubled by a serious knee injury.

'I don't understand it at all because her knee got better. Whether that was psychological—God created psychology anyway—but—the knee wasn't totally healed, but it did get better and she could walk. The next time I saw her...she ran up to meet me. And I was just so surprised—and I shouldn't have been surprised... In a way that helped my understanding of the thing within me 'cos I didn't do anything. I just tried to be open, and whatever happened happened from within me and not of me or through me.'

9
Going by the Book

I wouldn't say it was a book of rules because it's not...but it's what God's idea of living should be and what he wants from us.

Although different Christian traditions emphasize the special nature and authority of the Bible in different ways, all are agreed that it represents the foundation documents of the faith. It is given a central place in the worship and teaching of the church; its stories are the staple diet of the Sunday school; most preaching will take some aspect of the biblical witness as its point of departure. Young people committed to the church might be expected to be informed and knowledgeable about its contents.

It comes as something of a shock, therefore, to read their answers. The basic impression which is given is that of widespread ignorance. Of course most of the teenagers had some idea about the more familiar incidents in the Gospels and a few well-known Old Testament stories. But we looked in vain for evidence of more than a superficial familiarity with the Bible's contents. Almost no responses demonstrated what might be called a biblically formed mind or outlook. Our young people did not seem to have developed a biblical perspective nor to possess the knowledge of the text or the skill which would permit them to apply the Bible to a real-life problem.

We are not pretending that this is an easy thing to do. But the rhetoric of much Christian education speaks about the capacity to apply biblical teaching to life. A great deal of youth work is devoted to this end. If the enterprise is not to founder then young people will need to be confident in at least three areas.

First, they will need a more than surface knowledge of what the Bible actually says. No one could expect responsible application to proceed on the basis of a sketchy acquaintance with a few purple passages and a hazy misrecollection of some Old Testament stories. Was there evidence of a working knowledge of the broad sweep of Bible history—the story of the people of God—with at least a rough idea of the contents of the Gospels and, with luck, of the odd epistle?

Our interviews did not concentrate on biblical knowledge, of course, and this must be taken into account when evaluating the results. However, it was very difficult to find much evidence of a biblically informed perspective in the answers which we received. There were the usual comments on the early chapters of Genesis and some general statements about the nature of the Old Testament. But these were unsupported by more specific reference to the text and suggested that they were part of the stock opinions circulating in youth groups and classrooms. This is all the more surprising since a large number claimed to read the Bible regularly and many of these were following some kind of system. Either our questions did not pick up the knowledge which they possessed or they were exaggerating the extent of their reading or they were using the Bible largely as 'devotional' literature which may warm the heart but tends not to inform the mind.

This conclusion makes Mike's comments relatively unusual:

'I often found Proverbs quite helpful. I haven't read it for a while actually but it gets you thinking the right way, gets your priorities right, especially the first few chapters when talking about wisdom and looking for treasure such and such more than silver. I think that is important just to get yourselves right... I just find Romans and Corinthians a bit heavy going. I suppose, having said that, Revelation must be one of the hardest books to do but it's more interesting.'

Keith was provoked into more systematic study:

'My girl-friend did Religious Studies for A level so she was coming home and telling me all about it. And I thought to myself, "I'm not having this," so I thought I should have to read it now. Previously I'd read the Gospels and the beginning of Genesis. So I read it, the Acts of the Apostles and Genesis and Exodus and things like that.'

Louise was also beginning serious study of the Bible:

'I recently went through 1 Corinthians and now I've just started on one of the Gospels. I've also been through some of the older books of the Bible like Proverbs.'

But it must be acknowledged that these were the exceptions. Very few could match Liz, who referred easily to Job, quoted the apostle Paul's phrase about 'meat offered to idols', and the teaching of the eighth-century prophets in the space of a half a dozen sentences.

Knowledge of the text is not the whole story, however. Successful application of the Bible to life entails an awareness of the different kinds of literature the Bible contains. The 'message' of the text is embedded in different literary forms. Hearing what it says is partly dependent on recognizing that truth can be communicated in a variety of ways and is not restricted to factual narrative or lists of rules to live by.

Specifying in detail what this means takes us into controversial areas where different Christian groups give different answers. A story that is understood as myth by one group may be taken as history by another. However, it appeared that none of the young people we spoke to, from whatever background, had really come to grips with the principles involved. For example, the early stories in Genesis were often cited. But typically, the question resolved itself into one of literal truth. 'Are the stories "true" or not?' 'Do I accept them or not?' No other possibilities were on offer. There was virtually no recognition of the stories as vehicles of profound truths about God, humankind and the world, irrespective of their historicity.

'Some things I believe and some things I don't like. I'm not

115

sure about Adam and Eve. Like they had only two sons, so how come all the people in the world?'

'I think the Old Testament I find difficult to accept, but the New Testament although it's not modern, though it is dated, its beliefs are modern, and I think I find it all easy to accept.'

'I think a lot of the Old Testament is untrue, because, I mean, it was stories made up to teach people things that might have had a true basis. I don't think it's important to Christianity.'

'Like Moses and the burning bush. We were trying to put it down to the extreme heat in the desert, so that's what set it on fire.'

'Noah I'm not hundred per cent sure of, 'cos being a geographer, we've done physical geography, faulting and things like that, and it may be due to faulting or some movement of the earth that there was a flood in Noah's time.'

'There are still so many stories in the Bible which I find hard to understand and they're all Old Testament ones, like Jonah and Noah's Ark...'

'I'm just starting now to be coming off the Old Testament 'cos a lot of it's very...they're kind of kid's stories.'

The third requirement for responsible application is the recognition that the Bible's message is always set in a particular context. What it says cannot usually be lifted out of one world and dumped into another without distortion. Application ought not to be seen as a crude one-to-one correspondence which takes no account of the different horizons of the original text and the contemporary reader, otherwise the Bible becomes a magic book where 'answers' to problems can be 'read off' mechanically.

Jill had begun to see this and was developing some principles of interpretation:

'A lot of it you can translate straight into life, but a certain amount you've got to take a sort of pinch of salt, because they were rules and regulations of the time, and understand that that was written for first-century people... Obviously you can't go around living first-century laws... [such as] all the women in church have to wear head gear. I think this is because the ladies

of the time had to have their head covered whereas nowadays it's not a certain thing we have ... It was what God was saying to the first-century Christians and obviously to a certain amount it's what he's saying to us now. Through God we've got to interpret it.'

But again, responses like Jill's were in the minority. Here is another of this tiny group who took account of context when dealing with the teaching of the Bible:

'You're following Christ. And these are accounts of his life written by people who were there at the time. I couldn't just read the New Testament and then solve a problem ... I don't really have the problem of eating food offered to idols ... Paul would probably say the same things today as he did then and these things apply today, maybe not directly but certainly there's a meaning which applies today as it did then.'

The general lack of knowledge concerning the Bible and naivety about the way to understand it suggested that it was seldom read and largely devalued by young Christians. In fact, the opposite was true. A surprisingly substantial number claimed to read the Bible regularly. Thirty-two indicated that it was their daily practice, another thirty that they read it 'irregularly' and only five that they never read it at all. Of course such replies do not prove that they actually practised what they asserted to be the case. Nevertheless, there is some significance in the fact that they perceived themselves as people who took personal Bible study seriously and saw it as something central to their Christian profession.

This conclusion was confirmed by the not inconsiderable number, almost exactly a sixth, who read the Bible irregularly and yet went out of their way in interview to express some guilt about their failings. This response was not expected by the interviewers nor, as far as we were aware, was it elicited by any disapproval or surprise on our part. Reading the Bible was just part of the identikit model of the Christian and lapses from this ideal were seen as needing some comment:

'I haven't time. I know it sounds bad.'

'I read it occasionally. I'll have to read it more.'

'I don't read it as much as I should.'

'I'm very bad about the Bible. It's not a conscious "I'm not reading that" as I know some people have told me. I'm very happy to, and do on occasions, but I'm very bad about regular Bible study and I very often feel very guilty about it... I feel very guilty that I'm not [reading it]. But at the moment I'm not.'

As we have already hinted, responses exhibited another paradoxical feature. Linked with the guilt at failing to read the Bible frequently enough went a very high view of its inspiration and authority. Although the young people did not use technical language, they left us in no doubt that they believed in the divine origin of the Bible. Forty responses dealt positively with the nature of the Bible—a very high proportion indeed. They might know little about its contents, they might or might not read it regularly, but their view of its nature was entirely orthodox and traditional.

In eight cases their views represented a hard-line doctrine of inerrancy:

'I believe everything that's written in the Bible—the Old and New Testament...well, I believe everything that it says. I know this is my fault but I don't read it that much.'

Sometimes they qualified the notion of inspiration but still indicated a high regard for its message:

'I don't think it's necessarily the whole truth about the universe...but I think it is a good enough truth for mankind. I don't think it's the whole truth about God but it's the truth God has given to mankind to work on.'

'It may not be exactly what he said but it's roughly what he said... It is him but not exactly his words, not a quotation. If it's not what he said and somebody's muddled it up then somehow God's going to say, "This isn't quite right." Maybe somebody else will turn up with a different thing, and the person will think, "Ah, that's more like what he would have said." So the Bible is divinely inspired. That's something I've just put two and two together about.' –

Very often a doctrine of inspiration and authority emerged

implicitly through a picture or image or a statement about the way God speaks through the Bible:

'*I read a bit and it perks me up.*' '*It's God's word.*' '*God's handbook.*' '*God wanted it written down.*' '*God speaks through it.*' '*A gift from God.*' '*God wanted the books written.*' '*It's everything God has to say about everything.*' '*Through it you grow.*' '*It builds you up.*' '*It's God's idea of living.*' '*What's the point of making a cake without reading the recipe?*'

We might add to this the replies which asserted the relevance of the Bible to daily living:

'*The story of Joseph is still relevant.*' '*You can apply the Old Testament.*' '*It's bang up to date.*'

Alison developed this point:

'*It's full of the kind of advice that we need to go to today. To go through any kind of life really, for times when you're wondering what to do. I wouldn't say it was a book of rules because it's not... It's what God's idea of living should be and what he wants from us. So it's really his guidelines about how he wants us to live.*'

And, in similar vein, there were many who spoke about moments of revelation when the passage came ' alive' and God gave the text a directly personal application:

'*It's literally as if he's saying, "It's no use me shouting it out to you in a loud voice because I've already written it down."*'

'*He doesn't talk verbally but certain things can keep coming home and really touching your heart, and certain things are pointing to something wrong in your life or something that you must do.*'

'*Sometimes I'll just be flitting through the Bible and it'll pop up so that it'll catch your eye, and you read and it'll just jump up at you. You focus on that word and it'll just jump out. You know within your spirit that that's it. That's the Lord's answer.*'

What is missing in all this is the theme with which this chapter began. These young Christians read the Bible; many of them read it a lot. Many of them read it systematically—about a third of our sample used some kind of planned scheme or Bible reading notes. They had a high regard for the Bible and could speak enthusiastically about its divine origin and contemporary relevance. Even when their practice fell short of their theory, their theory was impeccable. But along with all this went a lack of overall understanding. They did not possess many tools of interpretation; they too easily detached the Bible from its historical setting; the notion of the personal relevance of the Bible was cashed out in terms of an individualistic 'word'. It is a slight caricature but, for most, the list of passages inside the cover of the Gideon Bible typified the proper way to use the Bible. These are problem-centred and context-detached. For many young people they represented a form of Bible study which was entirely mood-driven:

'I've got one of those little Gideon Bibles and I find when I'm doing my homework, say at school, I look up all the verses in the Bible which are on "weary" or "depressed".'

'I've got a little book, a New Testament thing, and at the front it's got, "If you're feeling worried or depressed..." all this. I look up what Jesus says about it.'

'I read it when I need help. If I'm unhappy or find things aren't going right, I take it out and read a few verses... I just open it and read whatever I find.'

'It was underlined and I went straight there and that was exactly what the Lord wanted to say to me. Words of comfort, you know. It was something like Isaiah, I think. It was something like, "Trust in me and in my right hand and I will give you strength." Strength spiritually and strength also for my week, you know, physical.'

'I think in a way it is a gift to ask the Lord for a message about something and you open the Bible and get a reference, a passage, that'll refer in some way to what you're thinking about or are worried about.'

There is of course a long-established tradition of using the Bible in this way. Our concern is that it appeared to be the sole model for so many young Christians. Certainly someone like Ian was the exception. He was one of the very few who seemed to be trying to relate the Bible to his work for A level Politics in an intellectually respectable way. He mentioned the difficulty of coming to a Christian view on such matters as the Warnock report, abortion and honesty in public life. He also appreciated the stance of his Politics teacher, who was prepared to allow him to discuss issues from this perspective.

The formation of a Christian mind is part of responsible discipleship. Whatever one's views of the nature of inspiration, authority or inerrancy, all Christians would accept that understanding the Biblical witness in its totality and with proper regard to context, is vital to the task. One area where this is attempted is in the work undertaken in school for public examinations. Fourteen of our sample were involved in this and their responses are worth recording.

The first thing to notice about Biblical study for examinations is that it involves a critical approach. This immediately makes it problematic for many Christians. The critical perspective on the Bible is often seen as dangerous and potentially destructive of faith. However, this is not the only possible response. For some Christian traditions the critical use of the Bible, far from being a damaging activity, is incorporated into the life of faith and becomes a central part of the idea of 'faith seeking understanding'. We were interested to see if this theme would emerge at all.

For some, academic study of the Bible was stimulating and raised questions but, as far as their answers were concerned, was not explicitly related to the life of faith:

'*I read it for study purposes for A level otherwise not at all... In RE lessons we have different views, different religions that believe in different ways the world was created.*'

'*I enjoyed Mark for O level.*'

'*A level has got me interested in parts of the Old Testament. I've read parts of it now.*'

'*My brother took A levels and we had lots of questions to ask my dad.*'

'*Because I'm doing theology, they've made me aware of the*

fact that it's not necessarily all fact. Not necessary that you should say, "This is true because it says this here in the Bible." It's just sometimes interesting and symbolic.'

Among those who came to their study from a conservative standpoint we could discern three positions. The first saw critical handling of the Bible as threatening and reacted with hostility:

'Sometimes I can get really angry with the RE teacher because she's not a Christian and she's very biased. She once explained all the theories about the feeding of the five thousand and I was so angry with her because I knew Jesus could do it.'

However, this student conceded that she had had to think through what she believed about evolution and source criticism. Her stance was different from that of the girl who played the academic game but tried to keep faith and study separate:

'The teacher who took us was definitely for evolution. She said there are two theories how the world began. "The religious people think it is Genesis,"—for she knows full well I am a Christian—"and normal people think it is evolution." And at that point I just let it wash over me, you know. I didn't think about it. I just took down the notes she gave us.'

A third position was represented by Liz. She was confused but not rejecting what she heard nor refusing to give it her attention. She was absorbing a lot of what she was being taught and trying, at the same time, to integrate it with her basic conservatism:

'The creation story. I think maybe now I would say it's not literal... Yes, this has mainly come from my A level studies. As for things in the Gospels, I believe that they happened but perhaps not in the order in which they were written... I can see that from some points of view what the writer was including was because he was trying to get certain points across... At first it [A level study] was terrible. I think I almost became unchristian because I was so confused.'

Finally, there was that group of responses which indicated that the work other young people had followed at school had actually helped them in some way in their Christian understanding:

'My Religious Studies has helped me think of God in a different light.'

'I really began thinking about it at the beginning of my O level course, when I really had the time to sit down and think and study questions. That course made me think about all the different aspects. It made me study myself, and also my church life... That was one of the O levels I enjoyed doing most, even though there was an examination, because all the time you had to sit and think.'

'The RS course I'm doing is literally pulling it to bits. Analysing it is what it's called but I often pick it up and discuss things because a lot of what I've read I'm now questioning. Look to see what is there, exactly what is said. I find this very interesting because it's making me think instead of just accepting what's written... It's strengthening some parts.'

And Gina was beginning to relate 'being made to think for yourself' to her doctrine of God:

'If you accepted everything in it without question, you wouldn't have your own thoughts and beliefs on it...just like you wouldn't be human. You'd be just force-fed something. But when you question it and state what you think is different, and you say I don't think or believe that bit, I think that's what makes it individual for God because every person has his own different attitudes towards it, and I think that God accepts that everyone's different.'

On balance those who experienced the systematic, critical study of the Bible valued the process for its capacity to make them think through difficulties and problems. It helped them hold together the intellectual and devotional aspects of faith; it integrated head and heart. But these were a relatively small number in terms of the total sample. For most the Bible remained a book of devotion in the sense that booksellers and newagents use the term. And this estimate of its nature is likely to perpetuate the 'lucky dip' or 'blessed thought' way of reading it.

10
The Cost of Faith

...although my Dad does not believe in Christianity, he said that whatever made me change is great.

...you have to a certain extent to sacrifice your popularity which is a very difficult thing to do.

But you might have been going out with a lass for a year and then she thinks it's time to go upstairs together. I would come out plainly with it and say I didn't want to.

I think Christians have a lot to offer. They have to show people real love, and that can overcome some of the difficulties that might arise.

Being prepared to stand up and be counted is always difficult. This is especially true if the views held are not shared by most people, or the side supported is in the minority. Typical excuses are that 'I'm not a good speaker', 'I'm no expert', 'I'm not sure what people would think', or 'I don't believe in getting too involved'.

Such reactions and comments stand in marked contrast with the attitudes and experience of nearly all the young people we interviewed. As we have already stressed, our study concentrated specifically upon teenagers who perceived themselves as committed to the church. We were curious to know whether, and how, they had made their stance known and, if so, whether they had encountered problems and difficulties. So we asked them all if they had ever made (or had to make) a public stand concerning their faith. We also asked them what sort of personal and social problems they had to face simply because they were Christian church-goers.

Their answers to these questions, and other remarks they volunteered during the course of the interviews, demonstrated very clearly that, when it came to living out their faith in the world, these young Christians really were at the sharp end of life. Not for them the quiet, comfortable life-style of many adult Christians, even when that sort of friction-free existence was what they really wanted. Not one of them found it possible to avoid conflict and hassle, some of it extremely uncomfortable and hurtful. Jesus warned his disciples that in the world they would have tribulation. These young people were certainly experiencing the truth of those words.

This 'tribulation' came in a number of ways, but it is worth emphasizing first of all that it came partly as a consequence of their attitude to, and concern for, their friends, their fellow pupils and their work mates.

Making a public stand

One question we asked was whether they had ever had to make some sort of public profession of their faith. Only five did not respond positively to this question, and one of them, eighteen-year-old David from Newcastle, freely acknowledged that this was something he felt he ought to do with his friends, but he'd 'not got round to it yet'. A number of others admitted that their first open statement that they were Christians, and went to church, came only because friends, or a teacher, asked them a direct question about this. Seventeen-year-old Mike was particularly honest:

'I've kept myself out of situations where I'd be called to make a statement in front of a lot of people. I mean, when it comes up in conversation with friends, I'll say... I always show that I've got Christian beliefs but I don't actually go on to say I'm a Christian, possibly because I'm shy but also because I just

don't...I don't know...I just don't want to tell everyone I'm a Christian. A bit embarrassed, I suppose. I don't want to go out and share.'

The great majority of those we questioned did want to tell others about their faith. Doing it for the first time was often quite an ordeal for them, and some, as just noted, only did it when confronted. But subsequently they were willing to answer questions, to argue for what they believed and to share with others, both inside and outside church circles, what they were experiencing at church and elsewhere. It was fresh and important to them. In all this, they were an encouraging example to other Christians. Even so, such sharing brought real problems for nearly all of them.

Not surprisingly, for many the first open confession was made in church, or to other Christians. Some did it at their confirmation service, or when baptized by immersion. Others were asked to 'give their testimony' at a church service, or at a house party, or at their young people's fellowship group. The opportunity for two others came when they took part in Christian marches through the streets, one in London at a public rally, the other on Palm Sunday processing in Peterlee. One boy revealed his commitment when he accepted the role of altar boy in his Liverpool church and one or two others said that it was when they read a lesson at a special service in church or at school that others became aware of their views.

These professions were costly enough to those who made them. Much more challenging and difficult were those made in less sympathetic surroundings. For eight of the people we questioned, these included their homes. Perhaps they were the first member of their family to become a Christian. So they had no idea what sort of reception they would receive. Two or three told us they were encouraged by the interest shown, but indifferent and hostile reactions were also experienced. Sheila, aged fifteen, remarked:

'Some of my friends have backed off, and my mum too. She said: "Oh no. I knew it, I knew it. I told your Dad this

would happen.'"

And life had been harder for her at home since then.

One Roman Catholic boy had to endure regular attacks on his church and beliefs from his father, while Melanie from Leeds found it lonely and uncomfortable at home because of her parents' lack of interest and worldly life-style. Of course those who came from Christian homes usually received a delighted response from their parents.

Christine, working on a job creation scheme at the time of the interview, went into great detail about her family relationships. What she said echoed the experience of others, and so perhaps a more extended quotation is worthwhile:

'They think it is fantastic how much I've changed. They can hardly believe it. Whereas once they couldn't trust me at all, not even as far as they could throw me, now when I say it's the truth they believe it is the truth. They have actually said how different I am to them, and although my dad does not believe in Christianity, he says that whatever made me change is great. At first he went really mad when I tried to explain to him. Then when I turned around and said I was going to be baptized he went really off it. He wouldn't speak to me for days and I said, "Well you're not going to stop me. I feel it is right and I've got to do it." So I went out and got baptized and I came back and now they are really accepting it. Now they'll not stop me from doing anything, even though it is against what they think.'

She added that she was now 'at the stage of bringing my mum to Jesus'.

The least encouraging environment for most teenagers was school. Listen to Tricia and Tom:

'Friends are a bit wary of you. They can make you feel inferior as though you're believing in nothing. It gets on top of you sometimes.'

'It's hard to stand up to people and say you're a Christian. At times you don't, and you feel really guilty, but you've missed your opportunity. You just have to say sorry.'

Seventeen-year-old Kathy from a school in South Wales told us:

127

'*I feel it's very hard in school because you want to be popular and you have to a certain extent to sacrifice your popularity, which is a very difficult thing to do.*'

And Penny from a London comprehensive said:

'*Being set apart from everybody else is difficult; sometimes you can feel really lonely.*'

Nevertheless, such feelings did not prevent most of those who were still at school from witnessing to their beliefs and seeking to persuade others to join them. They were ready to talk to their friends, help with school assemblies, and to speak up in lessons if the opportunity arose, which it often did. Kathy, whom we have just quoted, once took her Bible to school, with certain verses underlined to help her remember them, and engaged a mixed group of friends one lunch time. She was subjected to a fierce attack from all sides.

Nearly all those we interviewed spoke of being ridiculed, laughed and sneered at, told they were 'mental', 'stupid', 'cissy', 'soft', 'pathetic', 'a wally', 'Christian bastard' (many were called much worse names but declined to repeat them to us), and then either attacked again from time to time, or simply shunned. Some of their non-Christian friends did, after a time, accept that they had different values and left things at that. But as Derek from Washington commented, 'The ridicule is sometimes hard to take.' He added: 'Not 'cos I'm scared, but 'cos they're ignorant' [about what they were mocking]. Steve summed up the problem this way:

'*They think we are weird 'cos we can stand up and talk about it.*'

Those young people at work or on the dole also faced their share of prejudice and contempt. Nevertheless, this usually did not prevent them from speaking about their beliefs and against some of the practices they met with. One youth tackled the chef in the hotel where he worked for his constant blasphemy. Another refused to obey the shop manager's order to mislead customers if necessary, in order to sell goods. Others refused to take part in lunch time activities which they saw could compromise their faith. And like their

128

counterparts in school, they would use and try to create opportunities to talk about the Christian faith, from time to time.

Social problems

Towards the end of each interview, we asked all the teenagers whether they had experienced any social or personal problems, simply because they were Christians. Only four of the whole sample answered this question in the negative. Most young people gave us several examples of such difficulties. For convenience they may be simply grouped under two headings, problems from without, and problems from within. Both sorts had to be faced for two reasons at least. One, already referred to, was that their real desire to share their faith and experiences produced reactions difficult to handle. The other was the simple fact of living in the world where Christian beliefs and values are either ignored or vilified. There is also the fact that, as adolescents, all the young people we met were still coming to terms with themselves, with others and with life.

Problems from without
From what we were told, easily the most constant difficulty they faced was mockery. It is neither easy nor pleasant regularly to be labelled boring, stupid or wet. Many of the young people we met pointed out that they had not been Christians for very long. They found it equally distressing to hear their new-found faith and interests scorned and misrepresented as pointless, misguided, ridiculous, a sort of thou-shalt-not lifestyle, and so on.

But it was harder still to have to give up or to lose friends because of Christian commitment. As it became clearer to them that they had changed or were changing, that they were at a fundamental level different from their companions, so they had to try to adjust to this new situation. How they were doing this varied, just as their personal circumstances varied. But none of them found it easy.

Sometimes it involved outright rejection. Boy-and-girl friendships broke up, or individuals found they were no longer accepted as members of the group or the 'in-crowd'. As they changed their habits—regular drinking, glue sniffing, wild party going, Sunday football and hair dyeing were all given as examples—so they found themselves no longer a part of their familiar social scene. They usually did not mind changing their activities, but it was still hard to lose friends whose company they enjoyed.

More frequently they described a gradual drifting away from former friends, a cooling not easy to come to terms with unless the loss on one side was made up by the making of new friends at church or the Christian youth group. Happily most of our sample did find new friends, or came to make friends with Christian young people they already knew but with whom they'd had little close contact. Paul's answer illustrates the experience of many:

'*I now find it hard to socialize. I can socialize with my friends at work but I'm very diffident, and aware of it. I don't say "I'm not going to drink with you," or "I'm not going out with you because you lot are not Christians," because that would be a totally wrong attitude. Some Christians believe that if you're a Christian you should only go around with Christians, but I don't believe that. I mean, how can you witness if you don't go with them? I believe you have to go along with some of the things they do. But there is an uneasiness about it.*'

After mockery and friendship changes, most of the other social problems facing young Christians can be summed up under the heading of 'doing what everybody else does'. The pressure to conform to the standards and life-style of one's social group is felt by most people of all ages and creeds. It is probably true to say that young people feel this pressure more than anyone else. To go along with what everyone else appears to be doing or saying is regarded as normal, perfectly natural and wholly acceptable. To stand apart therefore is not only very difficult; it makes one very conspicuous. For adolescents, already more than prone to self-consciousness, to be seen to be different from their peers is a tremendous challenge.

For example, party going is a very popular pastime with all young people, Christian young people included. But the nature of many of these social evenings worried the teenagers we talked to. Many refused to go at all with their non-Christian friends. Those who did go said they often sat apart from the rest, preferring simply to talk and drink orange juice rather than the alcohol which was usually available. Going out drinking is another popular activity for both sexes from which our Christian contacts now withdrew in most cases. Listening to certain kinds of pop music—hard rock and heavy metal groups were cited—also provided a challenge for a number of them. Several who played as well as listened to such music felt it necessary to stop, usually because of what they saw as the unwholesome and sometimes satanic messages conveyed by both words and music.

But let the young people speak for themselves. Here's Rebecca:

'Obviously, when I've been invited to a party, it's difficult to know whether to go or not. And if I do go, what am I supposed to do? Because everyone else will be drinking or whatever, and I just sit there and think, "What on earth am I supposed to be doing?" Or if they go out on the town. I don't know if it is because I'm a Christian or that I just don't like going out on the town at night. I feel that's quite difficult.'

Emma's views on drinking revealed the problem she faced:

'Before I made my commitment I really used to look forward to going out for a drink. I drank too much. And now I think I've been out a couple of times since then...it is something I've got to pray about. Even ask for healing about. I don't know. It's a sort of battle.'

Martin also thought that drinking was a serious issue that he had to resolve:

'Well, I feel that at the moment it's the in thing to drink, even under age. It's been a very big temptation to go out drinking with friends, and as a Christian I don't think I should do that because, as I say, I'm under age and my dad has taught us not to drink. I don't drink and therefore there is a conflict, because if somebody offers me a drink and I refuse, they wonder why, and if they're not in a fit state to understand, they go and mock and do this, that and the other.'

Tim provided some intriguing views on the subject of music:

'Only those who know me really well realize how much a part of my life music is. And I've been challenged very much recently because of how Satan really just got hold of the music business. I mean that really has made a major revolution in an area of my life which is very close to me, because I've had to say "No" to certain records and to certain pieces that I can play on my guitar. And that has been very difficult, especially at the beginning, but now, I won't say I've got it completely sussed because something's bound to come up, but I'm getting over it.'

Another commonly felt problem concerned going out with members of the opposite sex. Steve spoke with great feeling on the subject:

'The Lord commands you not to have sex before marriage and it's really hard. It's really...well, it's hard! That's where I find it really difficult, 'cos in the environment I was brought up in, it's the natural thing. That's the way the devil's brought it out—to make it natural. But it's unnatural. I've been with lasses that aren't Christian—and people say you can change them into being a Christian...but with me it's been the other way round. They've pulled me down. And I'm just sick of that happening. And I don't want it to happen again. I don't want to mix with darkness.'

His way of solving the problem was to pray for a Christian lass:

'And I wouldn't marry a lass unless the Lord said it was the right one. 'Cos I know it'd be a complete mix up.'

Barry's problem was perhaps made even more difficult

because girls found him very attractive. He liked their company:

'But if one comes on a bit strong, then I'll refuse and that's the time to tell her. Tell her what you are. Some of my mates will say, "Oh, he's a bit funny," but never mind. People used to think I was bent... But you might have been going out with a lass for a year and then she thinks it's time to go upstairs together. I would come out plainly with it and say I didn't want to. But it's not easy.'

Emma likewise shared a reaction that other female teenagers also referred to:

'Once if somebody asked me out, I couldn't say no. It was too good to miss. But as soon as I start seeing somebody, it just mostly falls flat so I don't want to see him again. And I know that's God saving me from that person because, whoever he is, he's not the right person.'

All these young people were realizing that to be faithful to what they believed could be really costly.

Problems from within

Many of the young people commented on the difficulty of mastering temptation in its different forms. The temptation to go along with the crowd, even before invitations had been extended, was always present. Ed confessed that temptations were his biggest social and personal problem:

'...temptations of life in general, like shall I go to a party and get drunk? There are classic things that I would definitely not do, like should I break a house window, or steal a car? No, it's the little things, sort of the devil creeping in and getting you— should I go with this girl, or beat this person up 'cos I don't like him, or should I lose my temper again? It's just temptations in life.'

David outlined the struggle more precisely:

'Sometimes you can be given exactly the same temptation but just in the right situation you simply say no, so you don't want it. But at other times I might think, "Oh, I wouldn't mind having that." I often have these little pacts with God and I say, "Right,

133

*for one week I'm not going to do this, to drink or whatever." I
usually do it over a seven day period, not for any particular
purpose but just for the sake of it. But I'll often do that. That
gives me extra strength and you can almost hear yourself saying,
"Oh, come on, why not do that?" but I'm not going to deny him.
It may be the sixth day and another voice comes, "Oh come on,
why not do it?" but you say, "No. Get out."'*

The other main 'problem from within' related to their
efforts to think and believe in a more Christian way. A
number of girls referred to the temptation to gossip and to
criticize others. A few of the boys also alerted themselves—
and us—to the danger of sitting in judgment on others.
Several said they found trying to live by God's laws difficult
at times, and they instanced telling lies, answering back,
losing self control, wanting to swear at or to mock those who
mocked them. One girl complained:

*'There's not enough said to you about Christianity and
temptations and pressures, and what being a Christian really
entails.'*

Andy felt that the church—or his denomination at least—
sat on the fence on too many issues, a situation which he
thought too many Christians simply accepted, making him
feel somewhat isolated even within the church.

Yet it would be wrong to imply that their personal and
social problems as Christians left them wholly downhearted
or negative-minded. Far from it. They left us in no doubt that
they suffered in many ways for their commitment, but they
had positive advice to give as well. Seventeen-year-old Elaine
made this declaration:

*'If you've got a strong enough belief inside you, then it doesn't
matter what other people think. It's how strong you are inside.
It's how much love and faith are pouring out from inside
you...you've got to rise above other people. Or at least above
what they seem, because most of the time it's immaturity.
Because if they were mature, they'd understand and respect
your feelings and why you want to go to church and pray and
things.'*

134

Harry commented this way:

'Maybe all you have to do is try to keep going and try to do the best you can, you know, as you are. People seeing that is often better than sitting for hours with someone trying to convert them.'

Mary had some very positive views on the topic:

'I think Christians have a lot to offer. They have to show people real love, and that can overcome some of the difficulties that might arise. They think Christians are finicky because they won't do this, that or the other...but I think if they see you as a loving person, that starts to make them forget about the things they might find a bit unpalatable...and they'll recognize that Christianity has what they need.'

We believe that these answers, willingly and honestly given to us, provide much food for thought. Happily, many of the young people indicated that they received help and support from their Christian friends, their clergy and older church members, in that they felt able to go from time to time for advice and guidance, most of all concerning Christian teaching on specific issues about which they had been challenged. We suspect that the sharing of their personal problems was less common. The blunt fact was that almost all of them, on leaving their home each day, went out into a jungle where violence and savagery were all too commonly directed towards them and what they stood for. Even when the temptations they faced were presented alluringly, the underlying destructiveness lurked close to the surface. We were full of admiration for the determination that so many revealed to persist in their faith and witness, and also for the concerned way they were facing up to their social and personal difficulties.

One great advantage that such problems gave them was that they could often see very clearly the differences between a Christian life-style or standard and that of the world they encountered each day. Certain values were thrown into sharp relief for them because they were trying to live up to the things they believed, and because of the personal attacks they often suffered as a result. Whether most of them saw this as an advantage is doubtful, but it seemed to us that the testing they were going through was helping them to grow as Christians. They were certainly more aware than perhaps some older Christians are that the normal Christian life is a real battle—because they were prepared to speak about their faith, and give a reason for the hope that they had as a result.

We feared that one outcome of all this for many of them could be that they were forced into a ghetto mentality, that the 'us versus them' experiences of daily life might pressurize them into a voluntary separation, even isolation, of their smaller Christian groupings. We were given little actual evidence of this occurring—only hints from one or two people at most—but we felt that the danger was there.

Let Caroline have the final comment. She showed in detail the way school mates and others were sharply critical of her Christian beliefs and church group. And then she said this:

'It is when you make your stand, and they realize that you're not going to back down, that you get your reward in the end.'

11
The Hidden Agenda

You do get pulled down the same roads, but the difference now is that you reach a point where you've got to do...where you're prepared to do the will of God.

It will have become obvious to any reader of this book who knows teenagers that the young people we interviewed were, in certain respects, significantly different from most of their peers. All of them were prepared to admit openly that they were committed to the Christian church. In answer to the question, 'Do you consider yourself to be a Christian?' each one would say, 'Yes.' That admission at once places them in a minority group among adolescents generally.

Nevertheless they remained adolescents and were faced with the business of growing into maturity as painlessly as possible. What exactly was the effect of Christian commitment on this process? Did it help or hinder? The question is far from academic. For parents who are not Christians their children's religious interests may seem bizarre, unhealthy and restrictive. They may worry that their son or daughter has become morbidly introspective or unnaturally serious. Their faith may look more like a case of arrested development than a positive move towards adulthood.

This chapter is rather different from those which have gone before. As we talked with young people we became aware that every one of them was dealing with a hidden agenda precisely by virtue of being an adolescent. Adolescence brings its own peculiar tasks. We went back over the transcripts to see whether the interviews gave any clues at all as to how these fifteen-to-eighteen year olds were coping with them. Of course, none of the questions we asked addressed this issue directly. However, as the teenagers spoke about their Christian belief and practice they inadvertently gave us a good deal of information about how they were handling adolescence with all its challenges, attractions and difficulties. Like other adolescents, they were working through their personal agendas—but in a Christian mode and within a Christian life-style. Their growth and development was being affected by their faith. Was this a matter for pleasure or concern? It seemed to us important to address the question, however tentatively.

Personal identity

We took as our starting point the suggestion of Eric Erikson that the central task of adolescence is identity acquisition.[1] 'Who am I?' becomes the key question and all aspects of life are expected to contribute to the answer. This means that self-definition and self-image become dominant. For teenagers the process entails the development of their own personal story and the formation of a consistent character through attitudes and relationships, the groups they belong to and the way they behave.

Does faith help? At first sight the answer appears to be yes. 'I am a Christian,' itself involves an identity statement. It implies certain truths about oneself and one's place in the world. Young Christians are almost given these truths on a plate. They are part of the package. Either the conversion experience or the consciousness of being committed provides them with an identity—and along with it the outline of appropriate behaviour and beliefs, and group allegiance.

The matter is a little more complicated than this, however. People may belong to the same religion but hold the faith in different ways. When James Fowler examined the sort of faith which his subjects exhibited he found a range of styles— some literalistic, others conventional, others reflective.[2] Some researchers have distinguished between healthy and

138

unhealthy development by contrasting the term 'fore-closure' with 'moratorium' and 'identity achievement'. 'Foreclosure' refers to a commitment which is the result of an over-hasty adoption of others' values. 'Moratorium', on the other hand, describes an active search for identity among alternatives, combined with questioning and experimenting. 'Identity achievement' marks the stage at which the quest is resolved on one's own terms, the stage of firm personal commitment. It is easy to see the importance of moratorium and identity achievement in coming to hold a faith freely and in a personal manner. Equally, it is easy to see the damaging effects of a faith which is nothing but the result of fastening prematurely on other people's beliefs and values without ever testing them or making them one's own. The first two are part of healthy development; the third is a way of escaping from the burden of choice and perpetuating childhood.

When we came to look at the interview material we were immediately confronted with the difficulty of probing below the surface of the young people's comments. The problem for the interviewer is that a statement such as 'God loves me and I am special' could be equally an example of foreclosure or identity achievement. We needed to ask ourselves some questions: 'How much evidence of personal thought and reflection did this young person reveal?' How much probing and wrestling has gone on? When Fowler carried out his research he found that, in the thirteen-to-twenty age range, about half were holding faith in a conventional way but over a third were on their way to believing in an individual and reflective manner. Our impression is that rather more of our sample were thoughtfully making the tradition their own. We have quoted enough of their responses throughout this book for readers to make their own judgments.

We grant, then, the difficulty of differentiating between premature foreclosure and mature identity achievement. We tried not to accept everything we were told at face value.

Nevertheless, the material did give us an insight into the way Christian faith was contributing to the process of self-definition, a positive self-image and the acquisition of identity. These young Christians were coming to see themselves as special. This was easier for some than others, because their home background and environment had been consistently caring and accepting.

This did not seem to be the case for at least one third of the young people questioned. For them, the Christian beliefs that God loves them, that he sent his son to die for them, and that he is always there to help and protect them provided their first genuine realization that they mattered and were approved. But for all of them, understanding their worth and importance as Christian persons was an ongoing and developing process, a journey of discovery which most of them were obviously enjoying.

Peter told us, 'You see, I don't belong to myself. I don't own myself any more.' Julie said, 'When I think about the past, I'm now surprised I am so happy.' Derek explained, 'You can be more cheerful and happy 'cos you know you're going somewhere. If I go my own way, it'll not work out.' And Mandy admitted she had a lot of failings but added, 'I have got confidence though. Not in myself, but in that the Lord is going to help me through. He is there helping me, so I've got nothing to worry about. And I now realize I've got certain gifts.' She mentioned the ability to organize and to make friends easily.

The overall impression they gave, even those most damaged by their upbringing and past experiences, was of competent, generally confident young people, reasonably capable of coping with the challenges and stresses they faced.

We have discussed identity acquisition at some length because it constitutes the basic task of the adolescent stage. A number of other themes are commonly associated with this period of development.

A time of hope?

We were interested in the general approach to life of young Christians. Were they basically optimistic or pessimistic? John Mitchell has stated that 'adolescents are creatures of hope and are not genetically programmed to resign themselves'.[3] If this is true of adolescents in general, is it modified or repressed in Christian adolescents?

Behind the question lies the fear of many adults that retreating into religion can be a way of coping with worry and stress. It is seen as an ineffective way, however, and may actually assist the downward spiral into depression and anxiety. In his massive study of teenage faith, Merton Strommen identifies as one of his 'five cries of Youth', 'the cry of self-hatred'.[4] In analysing the responses of over seven thousand young people he estimates that 20 per cent of his sample experience 'that worthless feeling'. At first sight here is evidence to support the idea of religion as a neurosis.

However, Strommen also identifies the 'cry of the joyous'. He argues that 'these youth have found a meaning system that brings order into their lives and gives answers to ultimate questions of existence. For them Christianity deals with the "really real" and supplies an explanation of "what life is all about".'[5] About 30 per cent of Strommen's sample fitted this category.

Confirmation of this optimistic view of Christian young people is found in Leslie Francis' research. He concludes: 'The majority of young churchgoers have a very positive response to life... 85% of the boys and 83% of the girls say they find life really worth living. A total of 73% "feel my life had a sense of purpose".'[6]

In our view this is hardly surprising. Christianity ought to help in producing an optimistic view of life. It offers a meaning system that is built into the universe. It emphasizes the love of God for all his creatures, and the supreme worth and dignity of every person. Central are the facts of the resurrection of Christ and of God's power to save, protect and deliver, and of the hope of eternal life for all believers. As we have already seen, in the replies given to us were a real intensity of feeling about the love of God in the cross of Christ, a very strong sense of God's providential care, and a conviction about the reality of heaven.

The most pervasive attitude they communicated was one of optimism, not least about life, about their future and their ultimate destiny. Their unquestioning expectancy that God was always there for them, always listening and always ready to help, had given many of them an assurance, and perhaps also a stability, that other teenagers lack. They could still be upset and hurt, and react negatively to events and people, but most were finding that being Christians brought the experience of hope and optimism.

Ups and downs

The adolescent is intensely preoccupied with the self. He or she is 'permanently in front of the mirror' and is excessively sensitive about the evaluations of other people. This partly accounts for their sudden swings of mood. It is vital for teenagers to have some objective reference which will help them come to a balanced estimate of themselves. When you are particularly prone to emotional highs and lows, there is a paramount need for people who will help you see yourself as others see you.

But here again we meet a possible objection to adolescent faith. Does belief in God represent a failure to find intimacy with a human partner? In other words, is speaking to God a compensation for the fact that you are no good at finding in other people the mirror that you need? This is one of the great fears of the non-Christian parent, that their child is going to become unhealthily introverted. After all, from one point of view prayer is talking to yourself. The conversation with the invisible person takes place inside your head. It pushes the transaction out of the public world and back into the inner world of feelings and moods. Are Christian adolescents opting out of talking to real people?

The reaction to these questions must inevitably depend on the reader's own estimate of Christianity. The issue is not value-free and our own prejudices for or against religious faith begin to get involved. For our part, we thought our teenagers were doing pretty well.

Of course, we noticed the self-centred nature of their theology. But we would argue that this is not necessarily a bad thing in terms of adolescent development. Other researchers have noted how God does become a 'significant other' at this stage. And this need not represent a move towards the neurotic. If the God who knows, accepts and confirms you really exists, then there could hardly be a more powerful guarantee of your worth and value.

Moreover, the young Christians we interviewed were perfectly capable of finding 'significant others' in the public world as well. They acknowledged the swings of mood readily enough. So one or two spoke of being sometimes 'on a spiritual high', which did not last. And others had equally transient times of doubt or depression. Tricia told us, 'You do have your ups and downs with God, but it's people that make it difficult for you.' Often the 'down' periods resulted from their feelings of frustration about their weaknesses and failures. What was significant for us was the fact that at such times they often found help by sharing all these things with their Christian friends as well as with God. It was interesting to note the large number who were willing to admit their problems to their friends and to trusted adults. They found that they were not unique in these matters, as perhaps they had feared. And, typically, they encouraged and prayed for one another.

There is no question, whatever our assessment, that for this group of teenagers faith was seen as a help and not a hindrance in dealing with emotional fluctuations. It enabled Graham to be philosophical about the subject:

'Sometimes you've got to go through bad things before you get

the good things. But if you believe, he will give you good things.'

Several emphasized the need to trust God in difficult situations, as Claire did:

'Often it turns out not as bad as what you think it's going to be.'

John underlined the fact, which most of the others confirmed, that faith had a steadying effect. In describing his commitment, he said this:

'What I expected was lots of brilliant things, but what I actually felt was peaceful, really peaceful, real deep down, you know.'

We ought not to end this section without making brief reference to the fact that a few young people do find that adolescence is a time of great disorder and violent swings of mood. Some experience psychiatric problems or attempt suicide or suffer from severe eating disorders. Does Christianity help such teenagers to cope? There were not many of this type in our research but there were a few and from time to time we have quoted from their interviews. However it may be interpreted, their personal claim was that their faith had changed them out of all recognition and had given them the resources to cope.

Relationships with adults

That most pervasive myth about adolescents—the generation gap between themselves and adults—has long been fostered by commercial and media interests. There is little hard evidence for its existence and much research which denies it. Nor need adolescence be always a time of storm and stress. Teenagers do need to test the boundaries laid down for them by parents and others, and this often leads to conflict in the home and elsewhere. It is part of their move towards independence. Again, the question of communication, both within the family and with the adult world, is often a genuine problem for teenagers and in some cases can lead to alienation on both sides. But against this, it is not difficult to cite numerous examples of co-operation between the generations.

The picture is hardly clear-cut, therefore. But it is still worth asking how Christianity might relate to these issues. The charge which might be brought is that Christianity encourages an excessively docile response to adults. Here, it is sometimes argued, are young people who are not being allowed to test boundaries or rebel against norms. They are unable to experiment or explore either because they are repressed by pious parents with narrow views or marginalized by an adult-dominated church or brainwashed into a system which restricts what they may believe and how they may behave.

There may be the odd example of such teenagers within our sample but we were more impressed by other features. For example, most of our sample seemed genuinely to like their parents and talked to them. The chapter *Someone to Turn To* has shown in detail that these young Christians had no shortage of good role models to follow in the family and in the church. They did not give the impression of being dominated or denied a hearing. Where they had criticisms many had been able to voice them, sometimes vigorously. They had plenty of opportunity to communicate and cooperate with adults, to assume responsibilities, to explore boundaries and share problems, to listen, learn and take initiatives. Indeed when one considers that the church is a group of adults 'on tap' as it were, young Christians may have a greater potential variety of constructive contacts with adults than many of their non-Christian peers.

Peer-group relationships

The importance of the peer group in adolescence is well known. What might be the effect on those adolescents who do not belong? For the most part, these young Christians were all very much aware that they were different, because of their

145

faith, from their non-Christian adolescent counterparts. The pull and influence of the peer group remains strong, however. Martin and Pluck's investigation of adolescent attitudes towards religion is pessimistic about the situation of the young Christian. They report the attitude of the average adolescent in these terms: 'There is a very strong feeling that going to church simply isn't a normal, expected part of being a healthy, ordinary adolescent... In general, they picture the church-goer of their own age as ultra-academic, a swot. It was a universal point made in every interview, individual and group alike, that an adolescent who went to church would be unmercifully teased and probably rejected.'[7] At first sight this suggests that Christian teenagers are going to find growing through adolescence a testing and unpleasant time.

We have to recognize at the outset that teen culture is powerful. We saw glimpses of this in some of our sample who were finding it hard to give up certain activities which they thought incompatible with their Christian understanding. We have already described many of the difficulties in relationships that being committed to the Christian church caused for all the young people. However, we have also shown that they can cope with such damaging perspectives. Not to conform to the values and activities of one's social group demands real courage as well as strength of character. All these young people had to exercise such qualities to some degree, and then to bear extremely unpleasant and hurtful consequences.

This may not be all loss, however. The young people we talked to had to tackle the problem of breaking some social bonds as they changed from being one kind of person to another. Their Christian commitment meant, for most of them, choosing new friends as well as new pursuits, and seeing less of old ones. This also meant that they had to rely on inner resources as they learned to evaluate the results of their Christian choices and to cope with rejection and attack from former friends.

Unpleasant though it may be, this experience is extremely significant in terms of personal development. Its implications have been helpfully set out by Tom Kitwood as follows: 'To break away, however, means a definite choice; a movement from the known to the unknown. It involves risk, perhaps requiring a person to rely at first upon inner resources rather than social support; and it is logically possible only in the light of reflection on what a person wishes to be or to become.'[8] As we listened to the young people speak we became aware of the large number who had made this kind of break. It was a testing and demanding thing to do. It also marked a great step forward in terms of self-definition and growth towards responsible maturity.

We must not give the impression, of course, that they were doomed to dreadful isolation by such a course of action. Their need to belong, and to be accepted, was being met through the Christian youth groups and particular friends within the church family. They were finding friends who shared their commitment, and many spoke with pleasure about the sense of belonging which came through their Christian friendships and activities. The big celebratory occasions which most church groups organize or support made them feel part of a large movement. Through these people and activities, their need for trust, love, respect, sharing, affirmation and acceptance was being satisfied. There is a strong possibility that this more than compensated for the breakup of other friendships, distressing though such losses were. They all had to cope with misunderstanding and criticism from various sources. As Beth remarked, 'I often feel provoked much of the time.' Yet most would echo David's assertion that 'being with close [Christian] friends makes it easier'.

Personal competence and achievement

Adolescents in our society experience confusion of roles, especially in mid and later teens. The process of coming of age is long drawn out. In other cultures adolescents are providers and fighters long before our young people. In some societies adolescence is unknown. One becomes an adult at thirteen. All this is connected with status and self-esteem, with freedom, autonomy and the chance to make real choices for oneself. The situation is aggravated when employment is delayed for many and when unemployment seems the only future for others. This confusion of roles and delayed or non-existent work choices contribute to another of society's myths about adolescents—that they are incompetent and hard to train.

One advantage of church commitment is that young people have many opportunities to discover personal talents and display competence in Christian settings. Belonging to youth groups, stewarding in church, leading a meeting or the junior Christian Union at school, organizing outings, being in a music group were a few of the examples we encountered. And in some instances young people who had been deemed failures in school were proving themselves resourceful and able in their Christian setting. This was particularly clear in the case of a group who met in a private house. Many of them had been school failures, on their own admission. Yet they were taking total responsibility for the social life, Christian study and worship of their group.

There were many others who talked confidently about the gifts and talents they had. Being involved with, and en-couraged by, others in different Christian activities had enabled them to discover and exercise these abilities, and so see themselves as effective performers. Such experiences helped them to develop and express their independence and to be their own person.

Values and ideals

Adolescence is supposed to be a time when values are explicitly and personally 'owned'. Even to state this is to raise all the questions of peer group influence and foreclosure which we have already touched upon. Some of our sample had obviously thought much about Christian values and could talk intelligently about them. Others, we felt, were still at the stage of uncritical acceptance. They might become stuck with systems of dos and don'ts which they had not thought about and which could restrict them.

There is the further question of the particular nature of Christian morality when compared with the way typical adolescents think about behaviour. The charge is sometimes levelled against Christian teenagers that they are too serious, too solemn and too controlled. They are old before their time and think too much about right and wrong. Certainly one thing that Christianity requires of believers is that they think about the application of general moral principles to specific cases. These young Christians often talked about the thought and consideration which Christian values required of them. But it is frequently asserted that on the whole 'normal' teenagers do not think out values. They live them out unreflectively. The problem may be particularly sharp for our working-class Christians. John Bennington, writing about just such young people, pointed out the problems which working-class converts discovered with 'all the brain' that was needed. Middle-class deferred gratification ('pray now, live later') was unnatural, as was the prohibition on 'having fun'. The Christian life-style seemed to demand solemnity and lack of spontaneity. He concludes, 'While the working-class young person is not afraid of spontaneous feelings and trusts these as the basis for his judgements and decisions, many Christians seem to get contorted in elaborate processes of self-discipline and self-criticism... The impression is that feelings are not really to be trusted.'[9] In the light of these comments we might suppose that being a Christian makes adolescence more difficult for many.

There was certainly evidence of moral struggle. Perhaps the most common cause of worry for most of the young people was the temptations they faced. They admitted that coming

149

to terms with being a Christian as opposed to what they were before was hard. Their struggle against their old nature proved difficult. Ed felt that 'it's harder to become and be a Christian at age fifteen to eighteen—it's the age you're at, when everything can go against you'. He explained that there were just too many temptations at this period of one's life. Beth said:

'You do get pulled down the same roads, but the difference now is that you reach a point where you've got to do... where you're prepared to do the will of God.'

She added honestly:

'Wanting not to do it is the difficult bit.'

Such comments illustrate Bennington's point about 'all the brain' which being a Christian requires. More positively, however, the Christian faith does give young people clear boundaries. In an age when fears of delinquency, promiscuity and drug-taking abound, it is worth noting the high moral tone of many of the young people questioned. Their Christian faith is clearly affecting their values and ideals. They have the role model of Christ himself to follow, and perhaps the example of older Christians in their lives. All would say that they have found the values they need for personal growth and for living out their lives. Several emphasized that biblical teaching about behaviour and relationships set the standard for them. As one said:

'My outlook on life is from the Bible's point of view.'

Derek explained:

'I feel I've got to give my best to God, so you can't really cut corners or start doing anything that's wrong. I have more commitment at work.'

Most declared that they were developing a greater tolerance and understanding of others, and we heard frequent expressions of concern for their non-Christian friends, even for those who attacked them. Emma explained that 'the things I used to worry about'—she instanced clothes, money and her figure—'I don't worry about now'. She said she was more concerned to help others to share her faith, and, as

Diane put it, to 'try to see everything in terms of God'. Stewart commented:

'Your faith makes you feel you should be doing something to help.'

Are they excessively solemn about life? Or old before their time? We have to accept that the adolescent Christian takes on a moral seriousness and a willingness to think about behaviour which may make life more difficult. Whether one discerns compensations or not depends largely on personal value stances. We did think that many had a somewhat naive and simple view of life—and perhaps people—probably because they were not yet really touched by life's problems and responsibilities. And some were confused. But the abiding memory is of a large number of articulate, thoughtful, attractive young people, refreshing in both manner and outlook. They exemplify Debby's summing up of the whole values issue:

'Now I've got something worthwhile in my life.'

We have tried in this chapter to look at the hidden agenda of adolescence as it is being addressed by young Christians. At every point we have been aware of the possible accusation that Christianity is ruining their lives and hindering the smooth progression towards adult maturity. It should by now be obvious that we believe that it is perfectly possible successfully to meet the stage tasks of adolescence through the medium of a Christian commitment. We concede that being religious in the twentieth century in the West does make for tensions. These are probably greater if you are adolescent, male and working class. But most of our young people were coping. Moreover, as we have seen, in some ways the Christian faith with its strong affirmation of personal worth, its clear world view and, at its best, its strong interpersonal support network is actually facilitating the movement towards identity acquisition and maturity. Some words of Hugh Dickinson are particularly apt: 'To know that one is loved by God and that God is infinitely mysterious is a healthy place for a young adult to be.'[10]

References

[1] Eric Erikson, *Identity, Youth and Crisis*, Faber, 1968.

[2] James W. Fowler, *Stages of Faith*, Harper and Row, 1981.

[3] J.J. Mitchell, *Adolescent Psychology*, Holt, Rinehart and Winston, 1979, p.116.

[4] Merton P. Strommen, *Five Cries of Youth*, Harper and Row, 1988.

[5] *op.cit.*, p.119.

[6] Leslie J. Francis, *Teenagers and the Church*, Collins, 1984, p.113.

[7] Bernice Martin and Ronald Pluck, *Young People's Beliefs*, General Synod Board of Education, 1976, p.17.

[8] Tom Kitwood, *Disclosures to a Stranger*, Routledge and Kegan Paul, 1980, p 256.

[9] John Bennington, *Culture, Class and Christian Belief*, Scripture Union, 1973, p.59.

[10] Hugh Dickinson, 'Jack and Jill: a Christian profile', *The Bloxham Project, Heirs and Rebels: Principles and Practicalities in Christian Education*, Blandford: The Bloxham Project, 1982, p.24.

12
Helping Young Christians

I think youngsters draw youngsters rather than...they're more likely to want to become involved if they see other youngsters being involved.

People think 'Ah, you're not good enough.' That's just absolute nonsense. That's the opposite of what Jesus says.

Our account of adolescent Christian understanding is now complete. What came very strongly through everything the young people told us was that their faith was very much a reality to them. They were all challenged by it. And for the most part they were really working at it. They seemed to be fairly realistic about the problems their faith presented to them, and delighted by its joys and assurances. They were equally frank about the trials and temptations they faced, and the difficulties that came from outside their Christian community, from their homes, their schools, their workplace and their non-Christian friends.

So are there any implications in our findings for anyone interested in young people? We believe some specific conclusions can be drawn from our material. Although our sample of sixty-seven was not numerically large, we think it was genuinely representative of Christian teenagers across the denominations. It offers a fair indication of the understanding, outlook and experience of Christian young people at this stage of their lives. As the Appendix makes clear, our selection criteria and research method do not encourage sweeping generalizations. But some comments do suggest themselves.

We know that some people already take steps to deal with the issues we wish to emphasize. We also acknowledge that some of the needs and problems of our young people are those of all adolescents, Christian and non-Christian alike. People should beware of the danger of assuming that becoming a Christian automatically meets the needs of adolescents and solves their problems, and that their parents and the church no longer have to worry about them. Some of the points we make are not new. We repeat them because they are important yet still sometimes overlooked.

We see two specific tasks where teenagers are concerned. One is emotional and the other educational.

An emotional task

During this period of people's lives, certain needs are crucial. We want to mention seven, which apply to all teenagers everywhere.

First of all, just as it is to be hoped that in the earliest years of their lives they learned to trust, so now they need to be trusted, even in making their own mistakes. The temptation always to control and manipulate them must be resisted.

Second, they need to be loved unconditionally. They have always needed this, but such love and acceptance become even more important when they are trying to be free.

That leads to the third need—for independence, to be their own person, for at least some autonomy in their lives.

Fourth, they need explicit affirmation, not least that which is based on respect for what they want to do. Advice and guidance are appreciated when they know the respect is clearly there.

Next, they need to be allowed to communicate, and to be listened to.

This mutual sharing and listening applies also to the sixth need, for increasing responsibility, not least for their own moral lives. Where rules are necessary, sharing in rule formation is important.

Last, they need to be cut free emotionally. Those who are most involved with them have to let them go.

In chapter one, we said we thought our book was especially relevant to three groups of people—parents who are not religious, parents who are Christians, and those in the church who are involved with young people. What part should they all play, in the light of these things?

The role of parents

By far the most important point for anyone interested in children and young people, but parents especially, is that the young need constant unconditional love and affirmation. They must never get the impression, as some of the young people we spoke to did, that love has to be earned, or that their acceptance depends on what they do or achieve. They need to know for certain that they are loved and wanted, that they matter and are worthwhile, whatever they do. When they do wrong, they must bear the consequences. But withdrawal of love and acceptance must never be part of any punishment.

Most parents care deeply about their children and want to help them to grow and develop. While they may try to provide secure homes, care for the body, and encouragement for the mind, many feel that they are not equipped to help with the spiritual development of their children. Yet if they are truly loving, accepting parents, they are doing exactly the most crucial thing that they can possibly do to nurture the spirit of their young. Affirmation, praise, hugging, telling them how much they are valued, how proud their parents are of them, it is these things that more than anything help young people to grow up to have mature and healthy personalities.

Of course, some parents were not loved and affirmed like that when they were children. This does make it harder to live out the role model of the unconditionally accepting parent. But not impossible. They can still provide some of the spiritual nurture their children need, even when they do not feel able to give specific religious teaching and help.

155

There are very positive things they can do. After all, their responsibilities to be good parents are still there. The fact that a son or daughter has taken up a different life-style does not release parents from the duty of continuing to help them grow up. Teenagers desperately want the support and attention of their parents. So even if parents are not and do not want to be Christians themselves, they can still take an interest in what their young people believe and do.

They can allow them the time and space to explore their Christian world and develop their faith. They can let them talk and share their ideas, without being unduly antagonistic. When one boy's father learned his son was a Christian, he took the boy's Bible and threw it in a rage across the room. One girl's mother would go into her room when she was out and hide her Bible and Christian books. Another boy endured constant ridicule from both parents. And a girl whose parents were professing Christians was consistently criticized and discouraged because they thought she was 'too committed' in her faith.

Much more helpful were the parents of one girl who agreed to go to church with their daughter when she was to be baptized. Another couple encouraged their child to tell them what she was doing and to talk about what had changed her. These people were acting as any responsible parent should. After all, by becoming Christians, their teenagers have not joined some dubious, unprincipled group or club. On the contrary, their moral standards are now likely to be just what any normal parents want for their children. So support and interest are well worth giving.

The role for the church
As far as the church in general is concerned, young people need more encouragement than many churches and denominations offer. Too many of our teenagers, on becoming committed to Christianity, were allowed simply to join in whatever their church provided for all its members. In some cases, had it not been for certain individuals in the con-

gregation or in the youth fellowship, bewilderment and disillusionment might quickly have set in. Youth leaders and church people need to bear in mind that, as Christians, adolescents are still only babies. They need caring for as such. Hence, they need much attention, security, shelter, an appropriate diet and training, protection and regular encouragement. They need parenting and nurturing by the whole church.

The teenagers we spoke to were refreshingly candid and open about themselves. They told us of their struggles and reminded us that, like all adolescents, they have their 'highs and lows'. Even Christian young people, as Mandy from a Christian home and lively church reminded us, 'can feel lonely in life sometimes'. All adults have to try to be discerning about their needs, and about the stages they have reached in their Christian lives. Adolescents want teachers, clergy and youth leaders who are open, receptive and accepting. They need good listeners, and people who will talk with, rather than to or at, them.

We must say again that a conversion experience or a public commitment does not settle every difficulty a person has, or heal every wound. Christians would say it solves the most crucial question all people face, but many personal and social problems still remain. And that is where home, school, church and youth organizations could help.

Our interviews highlighted another area where all involved need to be more alert and supportive than some usually are. Many people come from reasonably comfortable backgrounds and enjoy a pleasant life-style at home, at church, and elsewhere. We were made uncomfortably aware by many of those interviewed that we had little conception of what they had to go through day by day. Young people who admit openly that they are Christians usually have to endure constant pressures and persecution which are both oppressive and frightening. Adults need to be alive to this and provide the backing and help required to cope with such difficulties.

But the truth is that not all parents, teachers, friends and clergy fully understand the needs of the young. Nor are they all as sensitive to these needs as they should be. Some of what we have quoted draws attention to parents, clergy and church leaders who were not very understanding or helpful.

So how might adults respond to these matters? In addition to the general points we are making, we offer two practical suggestions.

First, teenagers want people who will share with them. This is often best done in a home setting. They want people to welcome them to their homes and provide them with friendship. This is true of them all but may be especially needful for teenagers from deprived backgrounds. Steve's comment makes this point eloquently:

'I honestly believe more Christians should open up their homes to the young. Just somewhere they can go, be themselves, identify with each other, and just grow in the Lord. It takes a lot for a kid up our street to go to church. 'Cos if you can't go to school or a church, a home's the only place you can go to.'

Second, like all growing children, they need people to identify with. For the young people we interviewed, that would include Christians who model their faith as well as teach it. And it is worth remembering that while most of them do want to share, to talk, to ask questions, they don't always want to do those things with their parents or the clergy, even when they are sympathetic and approachable.

We are conscious that our second suggestion is an ideal, and not always easy to act upon. That is, to provide each new young Christian with a couple of church 'parents' who would watch over their progress and be a source of comfort and support. Youth leaders often fulfil this task. Our guess is that teenagers might respond best to those who are no more than ten to fifteen years older than themselves, people they would probably still class as 'modern' and in touch with their world. But older couples could equally be the right ones for some adolescents. The 'parenting' may well also have to be done for much of the time in smallish groups, rather than solely on an individual basis, though opportunities for personal counselling should always be there as well.

We think it worth listing some of the problems to which our young people referred most frequently. Underneath the masks they too often put on for the world, there are real fears—about themselves, about being accepted, about how they will cope in the different situations life throws up for them. Perhaps the most common problem concerns how to sort out relationships of all kinds in a Christian way. Then there are problems of coping with guilt and with failures. They also all have doubts from time to time about their faith and about themselves, and they need to share these without fear of criticism. Being a Christian is not all plain sailing for them, especially in the low periods. They are tempted at times to rebel.

Anne commented:

'It's hard to be always on your toes. You feel like you should do everything well.'

All too often the fear behind such a remark is that they will only be accepted if they 'do everything well'. Christian teaching itself explains that believers do not have to keep earning acceptance by strict obedience to the law. Like forgiveness, it is given through God's grace, and they need much reminding of the fact.

Some young people go through depths of suffering, feeling worthless, helpless, and even unwanted—all a heritage from their past that is not easily healed or overcome. From our group, Penny confessed:

'I didn't have the courage to go and talk to people because I didn't accept myself, because I didn't love myself.'

A few have problems about non-Christian boy- and girl-friends, and having to give up such friends sometimes because of their social life-style. Coping with friends who do not understand their change in values and behaviour can be hard and painful, and among other things creates the need for more affirmation by the church. And there are still the

159

temptations common to adolescents generally today—alcohol, sexual relationships, drugs, gossip and swearing.

Many told us of problems they faced before they became Christians. Fear of death, bad dreams, suicidal feelings, self-dislike, feeling they were failures, or, in several cases, feeling they could do anything, were all mentioned. Helping them to voice these problems is clearly important. And such difficulties do not go away the moment a Christian commitment has been made. Barry said this:

'I felt as though—and I still do now sometimes—I was a failure at everything. Like at school where everybody, well teachers mostly, they used to call me thick because I didn't used to work my ticket at school. I started believing that over the years when they kept calling me thick, and so I thought I was a failure. I just really wanted to be on my own all the time, and sometimes it all used to get on top of me.'

Barry's words emphasize how much young people need welcoming, perceptive leaders who are able to teach and explain in clear ways. His words also warn of the ever-present danger of judging the young on the basis of external evidence only. Barry went on to add that what attracted him to Jesus was that 'he doesn't push us around, you know'. One of his friends told us about the people who ran the church close to his home:

'I didn't identify with them. They weren't like me. I'd have felt out of place going there. I'd have felt as if I wasn't as good as them. I did feel like it, when I went.'

We ask all adults to take notice of the young people in their midst, and to be available for them. The knowledge that such people care about them and are there when necessary is a great source of strength and encouragement to all teenagers. To have such backing when there is little or no support at home, when they are alone as Christians at school or at work, and when they are trying to witness to their faith is a tremendous help. And such love and openness helps young people to be open about themselves and their problems.

An educational task

Alan told us he had 'never had any experience of talking openly about faith' until we questioned him. We used the interviews to get the young people to tell us about themselves. But for them it was clearly a means of growth and development. After all, it is not often that teenagers get an uninterrupted opportunity to talk about themselves with the undivided attention of an interested and sympathetic adult. A number of those we interviewed expressed their gratitude at the end of the session and often made the point that they had never had such an opportunity before.

Some churches have a tradition of giving testimony. Often young Christians are required to tell the story of their conversion. Such an experience may be very helpful, though it is not without its perils, and the individual story may quite quickly crystallize into a standard 'testimony form'. But our interviews were not public affairs. They were designed to help adolescents articulate their deepest feelings and give shape to the way in which they saw faith and life interacting. The girl who said, 'How do I know what I believe until I've said it?' was stating a profound truth. Providing such opportunities would be making an invaluable contribution to the adolescent's quest for self-understanding.

Another crucial educational task for all concerned with young people is regularly to discuss with them the issues involved in being a teenager in today's society. The moral and social problems they encounter need to be faced openly and talked through thoroughly. This includes the nature of temptation itself as well as the activities which tempt. We were not aware of churches or anyone else providing special help with these matters. But we know Christian teenagers would welcome such guidance. It is a matter worth investigating, and acting upon where nothing is being done.

Last but not least, most of those we questioned admitted that they had problems in understanding certain doctrines of the faith and teaching of their church. As David said, 'When you first go along to church you are alien to those sort of ideas.' Those confirmed about the ages of twelve or thirteen usually admitted they were too young to understand and appreciate what they were doing. They did not always seem to comprehend that God is interested in everything they do and think. Aspects of biblical teaching were also difficult. A number said they found it hard to explain in words what was confusing them. They would value more help and explanation. Hilary, a Roman Catholic, made the point well for all of them:

'I think a lot more should be done to explain to ordinary Christians, to explain the meanings behind things. I don't think it should just be done for people doing A levels.'

From time to time we have made critical comments about the unsophisticated and limited grasp of Christian doctrine evidenced by our teenagers. It is neither desirable nor feasible to try to produce academic theologians in the youth group. But there does appear to be one area where young Christians experience embarrassment and where church leaders could be of direct assistance.

Debates and arguments about religion often occur in Religious Education lessons, General Studies or casual conversations in common rooms and at work. A number of the young people we spoke to found that they were sometimes at a loss to give a satisfactory answer in such situations to their more confident opponents. They occasionally spoke admiringly of those who 'knew their stuff' and 'could give a good answer'. Yet the topics under discussion were fairly run of the mill. Perhaps the church could help its young Christians to develop intellectually satisfying responses to such important questions and provide an environment which would help them to refine their answers critically and honestly.

This would rescue the church-goer from having nothing to say in the public debate and also from the unthinking narrow-mindedness that so often results from merely prepackaged

162

diets of 'right' Christian answers. We believe that young people would be grateful for such provision.

In their church life and worship, clergy and congregations could sometimes do more for their young people. There is a tendency to expect young people to fit into the long-established patterns. This is understandable. For the most part our young people were happy to do so. Few said that their church should change its practices just for them. But there is no doubt that some churches could make parts of the services more lively and varied. They could also make much more use of the young, not least in employing their enthusiasm and their desire for others to become Christians.

Most of our teenagers, though by no means all of them, wanted what Graham described as 'a get up and go church, not a sit down and snore church'. 'It strengthens what you believe,' said Gina, 'if it [the mass] is interesting. And after all, the youth today of the church are the church tomorrow, so why hold them back?' Many of them said they found it hard to be open about their faith at first. To use Tim's words, they would 'rather sneak out quietly while the going's good'. But this feeling did not seem to last long.

We feel we should also say that churches, whatever their theological underpinning and churchmanship, need to realize that if they ignore or play down their Christian teenagers' evangelistic zeal, they will be hindering rather than helping their spiritual growth. We were constantly impressed by their desire to encourage others to find in Christianity what they had found. They had a deep and fervent concern for the spread of the gospel. Churches must make use of this.

This was Sara's opinion:

'I think youngsters draw youngsters rather than...they're more likely to want to become involved if they see other youngsters being involved.'

163

Conclusion

What impressed us most about the young people we interviewed was the fact that, whatever their lack of experience, they were people who wanted to let God make a difference to their lives, and who were prepared to face the consequences of stepping aside from the normal run of expectations. We liked their freshness, vitality, honesty and simplicity. Their faith, whatever their background, was real and jargon-free. We know from long experience with adolescents that young people, including Christian young people, are not all easy to deal with, to help, even, sometimes, to love. But as we hope our book has revealed afresh, they are all special.

Of many memorable things we were told, we think Steve's assertion about Jesus is one of the most telling:

'The thing I know for sure is that the Lord forgives you no matter what you do—and he won't take it from us. Another thing is that the Lord accepts me for what I am. He picks the nobodies. That's something that really sticks out for me. He picks people that are nothing, like myself. People think "Ah, you're not good enough." That's just absolute nonsense. That's the opposite of what Jesus says. The Lord Jesus cares for the nobodies. That's something I won't forget. He picks the nobodies.'

Yes indeed. And as we think our young people have demonstrated in this book, he then goes on to make them somebodies of whom everyone can be proud.

Appendix 1
Getting Them Taped

Some readers will want to know more of the background of our research, the methods we used, the questions we asked, and so on. We set out the main details here along with some brief discussion.

In the last thirty years, there have been many surveys of teenage beliefs and attitudes. Most have tended to concentrate on teenage unbelief rather than belief. So our purpose was to aim specifically at teenagers aged between fifteen and eighteen who saw themselves as committed to the Christian church. A further requirement was that these should be teenagers whose parents, friends, school and work mates knew about this commitment.

Most research among teenagers has not considered their spiritual development at all. We think this is to overlook an essential part of what makes human beings truly human. We believe that no one can properly understand young people if this area of their lives and outlook is ignored, whether they are religious believers or not. This is another reason why we focused our enquiry where we did.

There is another problem about some of the research. It has been theologically naive and limited in perspective. For example, it has defined 'orthodoxy' in terms of belief in a personal God, a divine Christ, biblical miracles, and so on. This is useful as a way of identifying the target group, but leaves unexplored the richness and personal flavour of these beliefs for the individual. We wanted to find out what Christian teenagers believed. But the way they talk about their beliefs, and the language, explanations and illustrations they use are also important. It makes it possible to savour their own special personal approach to their faith. We hoped to discover how committed adolescents understood their beliefs. And we also wanted to identify those beliefs which played a significant part in their understanding of themselves and their world. We were curious to know how these beliefs came alive for them.

Again, we wished to try to draw out from them personal incidents and events which they saw as critical and significant concerning their religious experience. We had other questions too. In their thinking about God and Jesus, were there images, pictures and metaphors which were helpful, illuminating or significant for them? Concerning their religious practice, how did they regard worship, prayer and the Bible? What were the major influences in helping them to come to faith and to continue therein? And what difference, if any, did they think their faith had made to their life and attitudes?

Were there Christian people in their lives whom they saw as particularly important? If so, what were the qualities and behaviour of these people which made them significant? Were there aspects of Christian belief which at present they found difficult to accept? Did they ever doubt God? And last, we wanted to investigate the problems and difficulties, including practical and social problems, which they experienced in their understanding and practice of their faith. We avoided all hypothetical questions, concentrating on those which related to the realities of their daily lives.

Our aim, therefore, was to try to encourage young people to explore with us, in some detail, their Christian commitment. As we hope this book has shown, we think we were successful. It is perhaps worth adding that we were also interested to see what they did not say as well as what they actually told us.

The research was begun in 1985 and was completed in 1988. After initial planning and preparation, we decided to use the extended interview method, because this allowed us to explore in depth the answers we received. It also offered greater freedom to both interviewer and interviewee, encouraging them to be more relaxed in their questioning and comments.

We began by conducting several pilot interviews to test our questions and to refine our approach. Our purpose here, as with all the later interviews, all of which were on a one to one basis, was to get young people to talk, and to accept that they could say whatever they liked. We stressed that, as far as we were concerned, there were no 'right' answers. We did not want them simply to say what they thought we, or anyone else, expected or wanted them to say. We were interested in their real feelings and thoughts, not "approved answers".

It was most important, therefore, that the actual questions we asked were phrased as neutrally as possible. Also, that any follow-up questions allowed for negative as well as positive responses. We encouraged the young people at all times to say what they actually thought and believed, without commenting in any way ourselves. Even the few teenagers who wanted us to express our own views very quickly realized that we had no intention of doing so.

Each topic was raised in an open way and the young people answered as they thought fit. We hope that we have avoided—and that our readers do likewise—the danger of making interpretations on the basis of what was not said to us. For example, some chose to comment on the sermons they heard in church. It does not follow that the rest did not think sermons were important. We have, however, occasionally commented when no one interviewed made reference to key areas. We have listed the main interview questions in Appendix 2.

167

We also assured all the teenagers that though, with their permission, the interviews would be tape recorded, confidentiality and anonymity were guaranteed absolutely. We were gratified to note that, on every occasion, the interviewee very quickly forgot about the tape recorder and became absorbed in the conversation. We estimated that we would need at least an hour for each interview. In the event, that proved to be about right for the bulk of those interviewed. One or two sessions lasted for about forty-five minutes, and quite a number went on beyond the hour, occasionally well beyond. Each session lasted just as long as the young person in question wanted it to.

It was our intention to conduct all the interviews ourselves. In the end, this proved impossible since most of them had to be undertaken out of working hours, and also because we did not wish to confine our questioning to young people in the north east of England. Those who were questioned, sixty-seven in all, came from the north east, the Midlands, Liverpool, Leeds, London and Wales.

The interviews we could not do ourselves were with the young people from Liverpool, Leeds and London. These were carried out for us by three former students of ours, all mature and experienced Christian teachers. We had prepared a detailed interview schedule with equally detailed guidelines for the interviewer, and these were fully discussed with our helpers. They did twelve interviews for us in all, and these fully met the criteria we had laid down.

We ought to say that all of us involved in the interviewing were known by those interviewed to be, like them, committed Christians. This was important for several reasons. In the first place, this knowledge helped establish trust and credibility. Secondly, it allowed for freedom in the questioning. All the prepared questions were to be asked, but interviewers and interviewees were free to pursue other avenues if the responses seemed to warrant it. And third, our young people knew that what they told us would be understood from the inside, even though they also knew that we would maintain a neutral stance as far as their answers were concerned.

To share with a stranger their thoughts and feelings on such an intensely personal subject as religious faith, aspects of which are bound to be sensitive and hard to explain, is to ask more of people than most would readily give. But if the questioner is seen to be sympathetic and is known to understand and be familiar with the faith, and even to have experienced similar difficulties, then readiness to speak frankly is much more likely. Happily for us, such readiness was what we usually found.

We need to say something about the freedom of approach in the interviews, all of which were loosely structured with a flexible framework. Just occasionally, as readers familiar with interview methods will not be surprised to note, this caused problems, usually with those few teenagers who were shy or nervous—not very responsive for whatever reason. Before each interview began, we tried to put the one being questioned at ease, usually with general conversation plus some information about the interviewer and what we eventually hoped to do with our findings. But it was still difficult occasionally to get a particular interviewee to open up.

Sometimes this was our fault, not theirs. When getting little response to a question, we might rephrase it in too many ways, thus perhaps confusing our interviewee. Or we might talk too much and then ask a question which had the effect of closing them down rather than helping them to talk. Also, all interviewers were guilty in at least one interview of asking too leading questions in order to encourage a reply. Answers to these have been discounted in our final survey. We still believe, on listening again to these few tapes, that the personalities of these young people and their psychological state during the interview contributed to a less free-flowing session. But we think we also must share some of the blame. Fortunately, the vast majority of teenagers replied freely and easily, and often at some length.

As we have already indicated, our research centred on adolescents who perceived themselves as committed to the Christian church. We wanted to contact young people from various Christian denominations, and from all shades of Christian belief, since we wished to see whether denominational background and practice produced significant differences of response. We also hoped to obtain in our selection a cross-section of all social and economic backgrounds.

We did not believe that the use of normal sampling methods would provide us with young people who met all these criteria. What we did, therefore, was to contact Christian professional people from the different denominations who were known personally to us, the great majority of them teachers. We explained in detail the aims and purpose of our research, and emphasized that we were seeking to contact any teenagers who called themselves Christian. We made it very clear that we did not wish to be put in touch only with those known to be specially keen and active in their churches, or well able to talk about their faith. Indeed we did our utmost to find young people who might be described as ordinary church-goers. Nor did we wish to interview only those who went to what might be described as 'alive' churches.

This method gave us the names and addresses of a large number of young people with whom we then communicated, and from whom we chose our sample. We had hoped to interview about seventy adolescents, and our choice consisted of those able and willing to meet with us at the times we suggested. In all cases, the interviews were carried out in the place most suitable for the young person. In most instances, this was a private house, with a few taking place in a quiet room in a school.

Bearing in mind the purpose of our research, a detailed statistical analysis is neither necessary nor desirable. However, some facts must be recorded. Of the sixty-seven interviewed, forty-three were girls and twenty-four were boys. Twenty-eight were members of the Church of England, eleven were Roman Catholics, and twenty-eight were from Nonconformist backgrounds—Methodist, Baptist, Free Church, United Reformed Church, Pentecostal, Brethren—including four from house churches.

We were not given any evidence at all to suggest that the social and economic environment of these young people had any relevance for their understanding of their faith. Home background did have a significant bearing on the Christian lives of all of them. But the fact that in some families parents were unemployed, some of the young people came from single parent families, and a few were materially well provided for was of no importance for our survey. We were fortunate to obtain a sample which represented fairly precisely the normal spread across the Registrar General's five main social groupings.

We were a little surprised to find that some of the labels which church people and others use about different Christians and their churchmanship were wholly misleading, thus underlining the absurdity of branding people under certain headings and then assuming that this tells all about them as Christians. For example, terms such as 'evangelical', 'catholic', 'charismatic' and 'middle of the road' are regularly found in Christian writing and dialogue to denominate certain types of Christian belief and practice. They certainly could not be applied in that way to some of our young people. We are not suggesting that young Christians from charismatic, Roman Catholic or from evangelical backgrounds were not recognizably such. By and large, they were. But it would be confusing, and do less than justice to them, to pigeonhole them in this way.

From the language they used, and the Christian practice they seemed to be accustomed to, many might fairly be described as evangelical, yet they were associated with the most traditional of Roman Catholic and Nonconformist churches. The term 'catholic' might equally well be used of certain teenagers whose background was house church or low-church Anglican. Obviously, the particular church they were attending or had been brought up in had some influence on their understanding of worship and doctrine. What matters to us, however, is that they saw themselves as Christians, and that is how we have regarded them all.

Even so, it is worth adding that our teenage Christians as a whole appeared to be far more evangelical in their approach to faith than most adult Christians. We are not sure why. The newness of their faith for many of them, natural adolescent enthusiasm for a cause they supported, and the kind of teaching they were receiving might be explanations. But this is a factor which all who are involved with young people need to bear in mind.

In this book, we have, of course, made certain that no one we interviewed can be identified. The names we have used are not their own and we have altered any other details which might lead to their being recognized. Our transcripts also do not cover the rich variety and authenticity of the spoken word, in which accent, gesture, inflection and voice enrich the meaning.

It is also perhaps worth recording that, at the end of their interviews, many of the young people told us, without any prompting from us, how much they had enjoyed their session. We ended each interview by asking whether they had anything further to say, and whether they felt we had in our questioning missed exploring some aspect or element of their Christian commitment which they thought we should have raised.

Many said that our conversation had covered everything they wanted to discuss, and so they had nothing to add. But many others said they found the interview fascinating and worthwhile, because it made them think about their faith and their Christian lives. They remarked that they had never before been asked questions like these, and it was a real help to have to consider them.

One other statistic should be recorded. It concerns the answers to the first question we asked in every interview, namely, 'Do you know when you became committed to Christianity?' Eighteen girls and thirteen boys said that this had been for them a gradual process, whereas twenty-five girls and eleven boys named a specific time or period in their lives when they had 'become a Christian'.

All thirty-one of those who told us they had gradually grown into their faith came from homes where church-going had been a fairly regular experience for them. One or both parents, or another relative, had taken them to Sunday services, and encouraged them to go through the usual initiation processes such as baptism, confirmation classes and the church Sunday school and youth fellowship. Not all had followed this path consistently, or experienced all of these stages. All but three of the Roman Catholic teenagers had assumed that they became Christians at their infant baptism. And some of the Protestant teenagers felt as Mandy did, 'I came from a Christian family and so all my life I've known the church.' Most of both groups also explained that their faith became more real and definite later on.

A fairly typical comment was that of sixteen-year-old Beth:

'*It's very difficult to say. I mean I've been sort of a Christian all my life,'cos my mum's a Christian. But then again, I've sort of drifted off. I've believed all the way along but not continually, and at different times of my life I've believed stronger.*'

However, a few of our interviewees from Christian backgrounds had always considered themselves to be Christians until something challenged them to look more closely at themselves. Alan made this statement:

'*It was not until I got to secondary school that I discovered those in the school*

171

Christian Union had got something that I hadn't. Then I realized that there was more to being a Christian than going to church.'

Debby thought her actual commitment only came at the age of eleven or twelve. That was at a big rally led by Nicky Cruz:

'So that was, you know, the big time, although I had been sort of growing into it, being in a Christian family and everything. That's the time I put on for myself, for becoming a committed Christian.'

And for all those who did not come from a Christian background, it had to be some 'outside' experience or event which led to their conversion.

All thirty-six teenagers who indicated that they became committed at a definite point in their lives, all of them giving us the actual date or period when this occurred, recalled some incident which was the catalyst for them.

Two final comments must be made about our findings. Apart from slight diversities of emphasis or example here and there, we could detect no really significant difference between the answers of the girls and those of the boys, either in how they understood and regarded their faith, or in their attempts to live it out amid all the difficulties and temptations of adolescent life. Their answers are all personal and individual. But the factor of sex was not critical.

Nor, from the perspective of specifically Christian knowledge and understanding, was the factor of age. All the young people in our sample were aged between fifteen and eighteen. The older teenagers were generally more mature and fluent than some of the fifteen- and sixteen-year-olds. But it is important to remember that their maturity as Christians seemed to be remarkably similar.

172

Appendix 2
The Interview Schedule

Before each interview began, we gave a brief explanation of the project. We stressed that we wanted to know what they really thought and felt, not be given what respondents might think were 'approved' answers. We also stressed that confidentiality and anonymity were guaranteed absolutely. We then asked their name, age, nationality, church affiliation, parental occupation(s), and job status (i.e. school, college, employed, unemployed).

Eighteen main questions were asked, in the following order:

1. When did you become sure in your mind that you were a Christian? Was it gradual? Or at a specific time?

2. Can you recall any incident(s) which seem(s) now to be significant in your coming to faith?

3. Tell us about which person(s), if any, has/have helped you most in becoming and being a Christian.

4. What would you pick out as the most significant events or experiences, if any, which have happened to you since you thought of yourself as a Christian?

5. Tell us of situations, if any, where you have had to make some sort of public stand over your faith.

6. Does being a Christian make a difference—and if so, how—to the way you behave? To work? To life in general? To the way you approach the future? To your attitudes to other people? To the way you see yourself? To the way you handle personal problems and crises?

7. What Christian truths/statements, if any, really 'come alive' for you, so that you can say 'I really believe that. It's important to me'?

8. When you think of God, what thoughts, or pictures, if any, come into your mind?

9. When you think of Jesus, what thoughts, or pictures, if any, come into your mind?

10. How would you explain what Jesus has done (or does) for people?

11. Concerning services of worship in church or elsewhere, what, if

anything, do you find especially helpful or significant? What, if anything, do you actually dislike or find unhelpful and of no significance to you?

12. Thoughts on prayer. Do you pray? If so, how often? What do you think is happening when you pray? How would you explain to an interested friend what you were doing?

13. Thoughts on the Bible. Do you read it? If so, how often? If you do, how would you explain to an interested friend the point of what you are doing?

14. Tell us about anything else you may try to do to maintain or deepen your relationship with God.

15. Which aspects of Christian belief, if any, do you presently find difficult to accept? Can you give examples of objections to Christianity to which you do not have an answer?

16. Tell us of problems, if any, of a practical or social kind which you think you face because you are a Christian.

17. What are the biggest difficulties you encounter in having a relationship with God and in trying to live the Christian life. Do you ever doubt God?

18. Is there anything else you would like to add, or to comment on?

Age of respondents

The age breakdown of our sixty-seven respondents was as follows:

15	10	respondents
16	9	respondents
17	21	respondents
18	27	respondents

Social class of respondents

The social class of our sixty-seven respondents, according to the Registrar General's five-point scale, was as follows:

I	10	respondents
II	13	respondents
III	27	respondents
IV	13	respondents
V	4	respondents